NOTE BUSTERS™

Quick and practical exercises to master musical notes

Written & Created by
Karen Spurney
Steven Gross

Graphic Design by
Morgan Eveslage

top clef
PUBLISHING

Table of Contents

Introduction   v – vi

Note Reading Methods   vii – viii

Section 1 Exercises: Treble, On Staff   1 – 22
20 Exercises | 9 New Notes | Difficulty: Easy

Section 2 Exercises: Bass, On Staff   23 – 64
40 Exercises | 9 New Notes | Difficulty: Easy/Moderate

Section 3 Exercises: Grand, On Staff   65 – 106
40 Exercises | 18 Review Notes | Difficulty: Moderate

Section 4 Exercises: Treble, On and Off Staff   107 – 128
20 Exercises | 8 New Notes, 9 Review Notes | Difficulty: Moderate

Section 5 Exercises: Bass, On and Off Staff   129 – 170
40 Exercises | 7 New Notes, 9 Review Notes | Difficulty: Moderate/Advanced

Section 6 Exercises: Grand, On and Off Staff   171 – 252
80 Exercises | 33 Review Notes | Difficulty: Advanced

Answer Key   253 – 281

Introduction

Overview

NOTEBUSTERS was created to accelerate the tedious process of learning to identify musical notes for beginning to intermediate music students. Far too often, students become discouraged and quit their instrument due to frustration with note reading. Typically, students learn to identify notes with mnemonic devices or by identifying note patterns that frequently occur in basic pieces. Mastering sight-reading using only these techniques can take years, impeding students' progress and leaving them feeling defeated.

NOTEBUSTERS consists of notes that frequently occur in musical pieces but <u>without patterns</u>. Teaching students to quickly identify random notes along the staff increases their ability to sight-read. NOTEBUSTERS removes the monotony from the note learning process and provides students with straight forward exercises that only take <u>one minute</u>.

Guide to Completing NOTEBUSTERS

NOTEBUSTERS can be completed in approximately one year, working only one minute a day, five days a week. To accelerate learning, students can complete three to five exercises per day and finish the workbook in less than three months.

The workbook is broken into six sections that cover an increasing range of notes as the student progresses. The first three sections of the book cover notes that appear on the treble, bass, and grand staves. The final three sections cover notes both on and off the staff (ledger line notes). After completing the workbook, students will be exposed to over <u>30 different notes</u>!

Section 1: Treble, On Staff   (9 notes | 4 weeks of exercises)
Section 2: Bass, On Staff   (9 notes | 8 weeks of exercises)
Section 3: Grand, On Staff   (18 notes | 8 weeks of exercises)
Section 4: Treble, On and Off Staff   (17 notes | 4 weeks of exercises)
Section 5: Bass, On and Off Staff   (16 notes | 8 weeks of exercises)
Section 6: Grand, On and Off Staff   (33 notes | 16 weeks of exercises)

Each exercise contains 25 notes (26 in the grand staff sections). <u>Students should attempt to complete each exercise in one minute or less while correctly identifying as many notes as possible.</u> The one minute time limit teaches students to sight-read at a quicker pace and improves their ability to play music. When one minute has expired, students should count the number of correctly identified notes. Unidentified notes should be reserved for additional practice.

At the start of each new section, students should not be discouraged if their scores are lower because the sections are designed to increase in difficulty. As students progress through the sections, their scores should increase as the new notes introduced become more familiar. If students earn perfect scores within one minute for consecutive weeks, they may choose to skip ahead to the next section.

At the end of each week (every five exercises), students will be challenged to play the notes from that day's exercise on their instrument of choice. Students should aim to correctly play as many notes as possible in one minute or less. As students progress through the sections, they should be able to play more notes in the allotted time.

For Private or Classroom Use

Students can successfully complete NOTEBUSTERS in the comfort of their own home, because the workbook is designed to spark students' natural competitive drive to achieve higher scores and only requires one minute of attention per day.

Alternatively, the workbook can be completed in a classroom setting with teachers aiding in time-keeping and scoring. Students typically aim to improve their own scores in both private and classroom settings, but the additional competition inherent in a classroom is beneficial.

NOTEBUSTERS is ideal for teachers looking to supplement their lesson plans with systematic practice. Solidifying a foundation in note reading increases students' ability to grasp more complicated musical concepts and reduces frustration further down the road. For classroom use, electronic exercises are available from the publisher[1].

Note Reading Methods

Two basic methods of note reading are intervallic (relative note reading) and memorization (using a mnemonic device). Both are effective learning styles and most students develop their own combination of methods that fits their personal learning style. Combined with NOTESBUSTERS' timed and randomly generated exercises, students will have all the tools they need to become master note readers. For more information on intervallic and memorization note reading methods, see pages vii-viii.

Good Luck!

NOTEBUSTERS is designed to increase confidence and keep students excited about learning music. Students no longer have to be intimidated by hundreds of dots and lines cluttering their sheet music. One minute a day, five days a week is all it takes – after one year, students will notice big differences in the way they read and, most importantly, play music. Time to go bust some notes!

---

1. To purchase electronic exercises for classroom use, contact the publisher at orders@notebusters.net.

Note Reading Methods

For guidance, both the intervallic and memorization methods are explained in this section.

Intervallic & Landmark Note Method

Unfamiliar notes can be identified by their distance from nearby landmark notes. As students progress through the workbook, the amount of landmark notes they are familiar with will increase, and identifying unfamiliar notes will become easier. Beginning landmark notes are shown below; however, any note a student has memorized makes a great landmark.

Treble Clef:

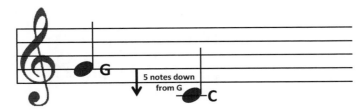

Middle **G** is located on the second line (from the bottom) of the treble staff, which is also known as the "G-Clef" because the Treble Clef's circular center falls directly on the same line as Middle G.

Five notes (two lines) down from Middle G is Middle **C** – one of the most commonly used notes on the keyboard and a frequent starting point in beginning sheet music.

Bass Clef:

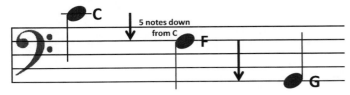

Middle **C** is located one ledger line above the bass staff and is the same Middle C located one ledger line below the treble staff (shown in the Treble Clef example above). Knowing where the same note lies on both staves will prove helpful while sight-reading.

Five notes (two ledger lines) down from Middle C is Bass **F**, which falls on the line that's surrounded by the two dots on the Bass Clef. Another name for the Bass Clef is the "F-Clef" for this reason.

Low **G** falls at the bottom of the bass staff and is therefore easy to locate and a great starting point.

Memorization Method

This learning style incorporates mnemonic devices in order to identify notes located on each staff. Both the treble and bass staves are made up of five lines and four spaces. Notes are located on each line and space for a total of nine notes on each staff. There are countless acronyms and other mnemonic devices that can be used to remember these notes, and the most common are shown below:

Treble Clef:

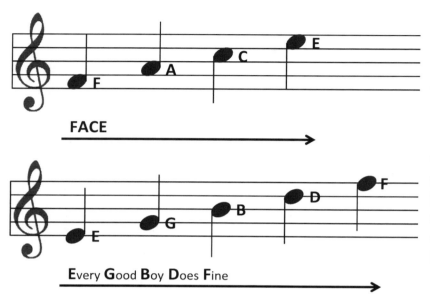

There are four notes located in the spaces of the treble staff. Starting from the bottom, the notes spell out the word **FACE**.

The five notes located on the lines of the treble staff do not form a word, but many different acronyms can be used to remember them. One of the more common mnemonic devices is **E**very **G**ood **B**oy **D**oes **F**ine.

Bass Clef:

The five notes located on the lines of the bass staff are G-B-D-F-A and can be remembered using the phrase **G**reat **B**ig **D**olphins **F**ind **A**nchovies (yuck).

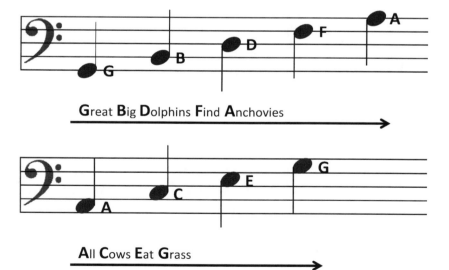

The four notes located in the spaces of the bass staff are A-C-E-G. A good way to remember these notes is **A**ll **C**ows **E**at **G**rass.

Using this method in combination with the intervallic method will help students learn notes above and below the staff (ledger line notes) that are covered in Sections 4 through 6.

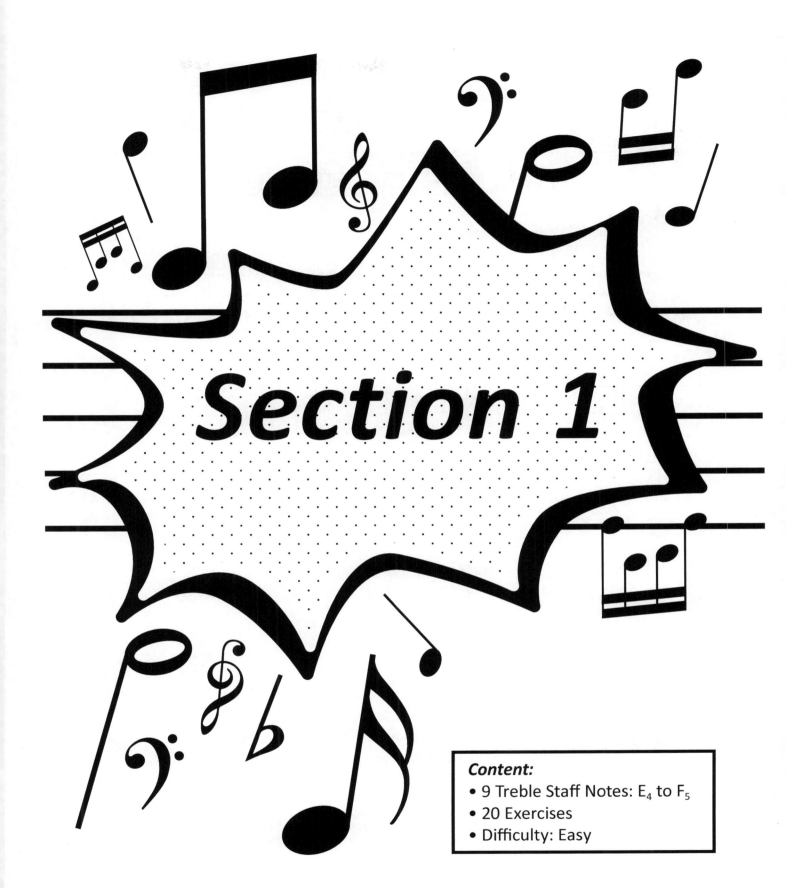

Section 1

Content:
- 9 Treble Staff Notes: E_4 to F_5
- 20 Exercises
- Difficulty: Easy

Notes Covered in Section 1

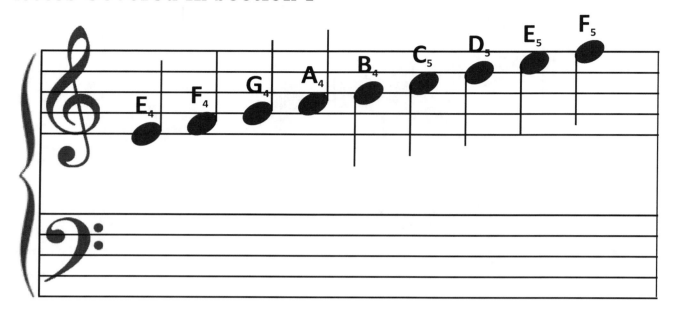

Instructions

1. Set a timer to one minute.
2. Label each note in the corresponding box.
3. After time expires, check your work with the Answer Key (pgs. 254-256).
4. Write the date and your score at the bottom of the page.

*If you finish in less than one minute, don't forget to check your work!
*If you do not complete all the notes in one minute, mark where you stopped and complete the unfinished as practice.

 This graphic will appear at the bottom of every fifth page. After completing the exercises on these pages, play the notes on your instrument. Allow yourself one minute to play as many notes as possible.

Need Help? Check out the Note Reading Methods section on pages vii-viii

Too Easy? Skip Section 1 if you are already very comfortable with the notes on the treble staff and would like to move on to the bass staff, or if you continually get all notes correct in less than one minute.

Completed On: _____   Number Correct: _____ / 25

1.

2.

3.

4.

5.

Play me!

Completed On:_____   Number Correct:_____ / 25

1.

2.

3.

4.

5.

Completed On: _____   Number Correct: _____ / 25

Completed On: _____   Number Correct: _____ / 25

Completed On:_____   **Number Correct:**_____ **/ 25**

Completed On: _____   Number Correct: _____ / 25

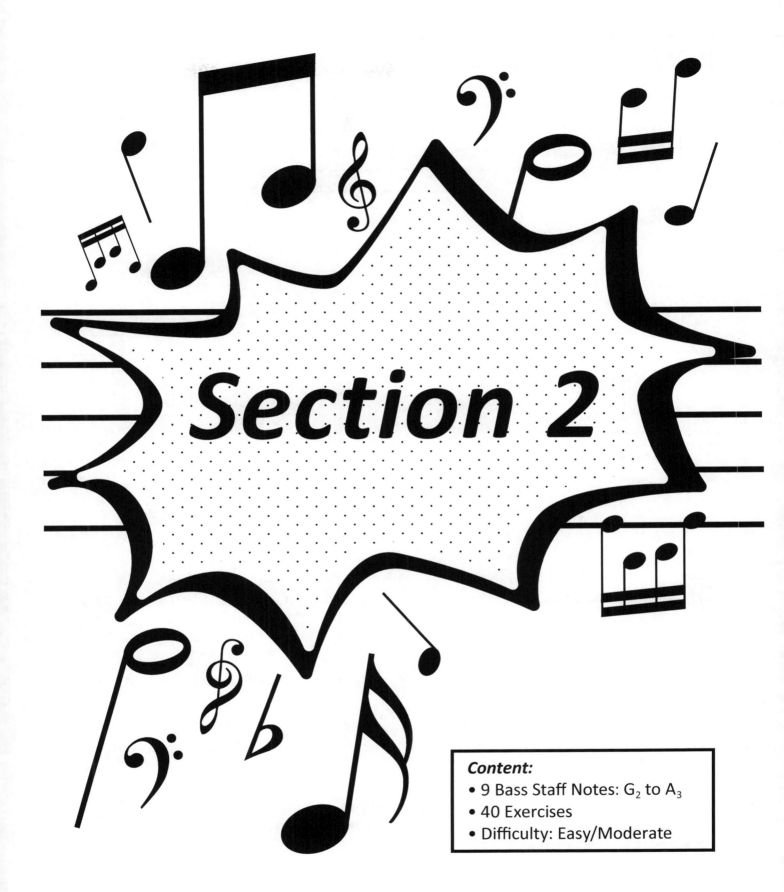

Section 2

Content:
- 9 Bass Staff Notes: G_2 to A_3
- 40 Exercises
- Difficulty: Easy/Moderate

Notes Covered in Section 2

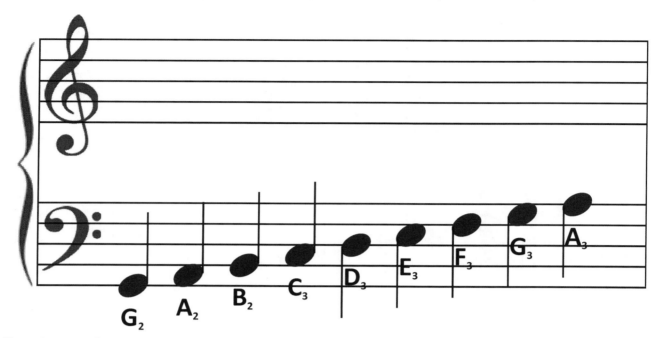

Instructions

1. Set a timer to one minute.
2. Label each note in the corresponding box.
3. After time expires, check your work with the Answer Key (pgs. 256-262).
4. Write the date and your score at the bottom of the page.

*If you finish in less than one minute, don't forget to check your work!
*If you do not complete all the notes in one minute, mark where you stopped and complete the unfinished as practice.

This graphic will appear at the bottom of every fifth page. After completing the exercises on these pages, play the notes on your instrument. Allow yourself one minute to play as many notes as possible.

Need Help? If you are not comfortable with all the notes on the treble staff after completing Section 1, contact the publisher at general@notebusters.net for 40 free electronic treble exercises. You can also check out the Note Reading Methods section on pages vii-viii.

Too Easy? Skip Section 2 if you are already comfortable with the notes on the bass staff and would like to move on to the grand staff, or if you continually get all notes correct in less than one minute.

Completed On: _____ **Number Correct:** _____ **/ 25**

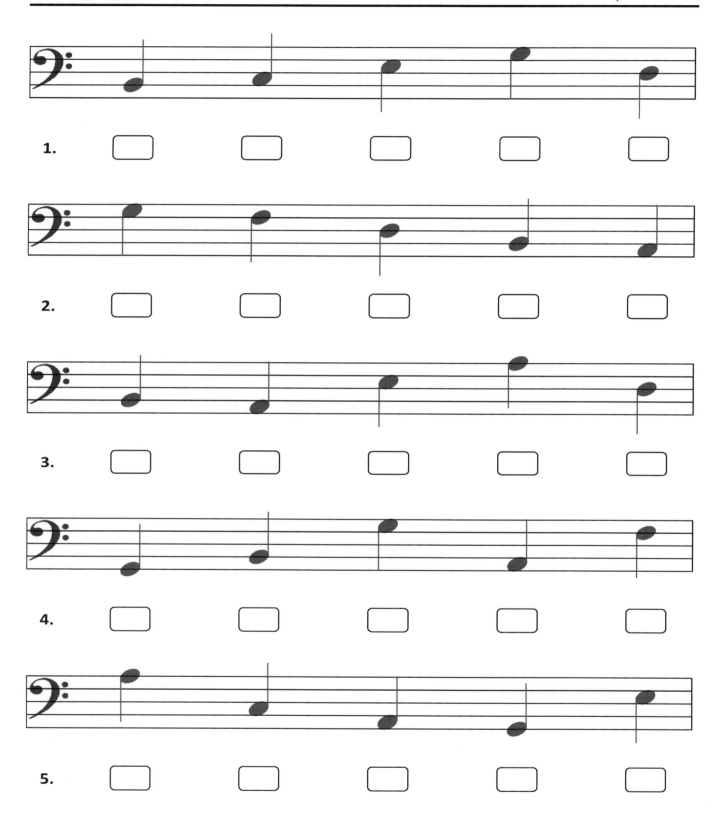

Completed On: _____   Number Correct: _____ / 25

Play me!

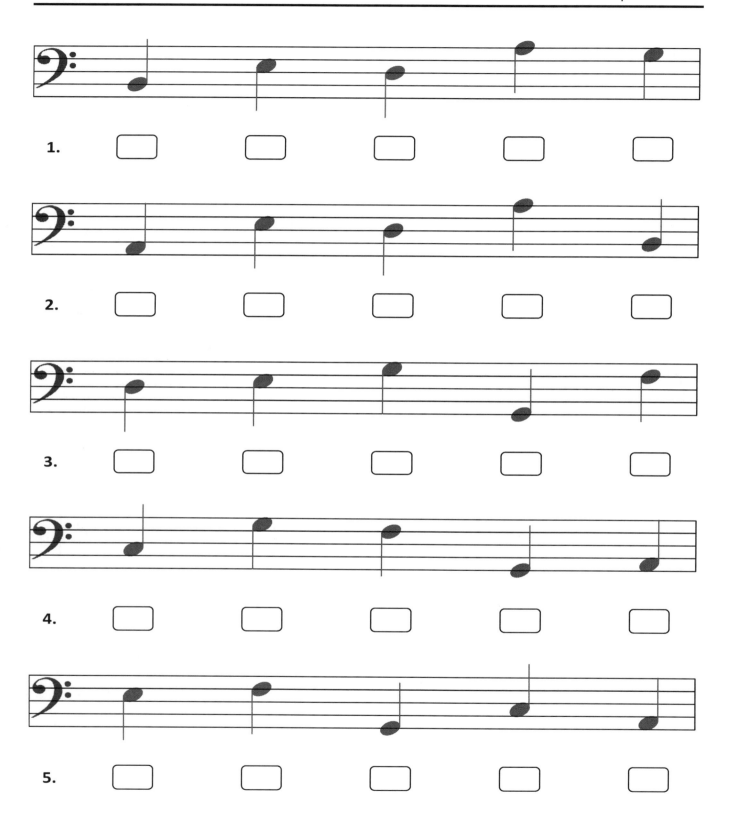

Completed On: _____   **Number Correct:** _____ **/ 25**

Completed On: _____   Number Correct: _____ **/ 25**

Completed On: _____   **Number Correct:** _____ **/ 25**

1. ▢ ▢ ▢ ▢ ▢

2. ▢ ▢ ▢ ▢ ▢

3. ▢ ▢ ▢ ▢ ▢

4. ▢ ▢ ▢ ▢ ▢

5. ▢ ▢ ▢ ▢ ▢

Completed On: _____   Number Correct: _____ / 25

1. ☐ ☐ ☐ ☐ ☐

2. ☐ ☐ ☐ ☐ ☐

3. ☐ ☐ ☐ ☐ ☐

4. ☐ ☐ ☐ ☐ ☐

5. ☐ ☐ ☐ ☐ ☐

Completed On: _____   **Number Correct:** _____ **/ 25**

Completed On:_____   Number Correct:_____ **/ 25**

Play me!

Play me!

Completed On: _____   Number Correct: _____ / 25

Completed On:_____ **Number Correct:**_____ **/ 25**

Completed On:_____   Number Correct:_____ / 25

Completed On: _____   **Number Correct:** _____ **/ 25**

Completed On: _____   **Number Correct:** _____ **/ 25**

Completed On: _____   Number Correct: _____ / 25

Completed On:_____ **Number Correct:**_____ **/ 25**

Completed On: _____   **Number Correct:** _____ **/ 25**

Completed On:_____   Number Correct:_____ / 25

Play me!

Completed On: _____   Number Correct: _____ / 25

Completed On:_____   Number Correct:_____ / 25

Completed On:_____   **Number Correct:**_____ **/ 25**

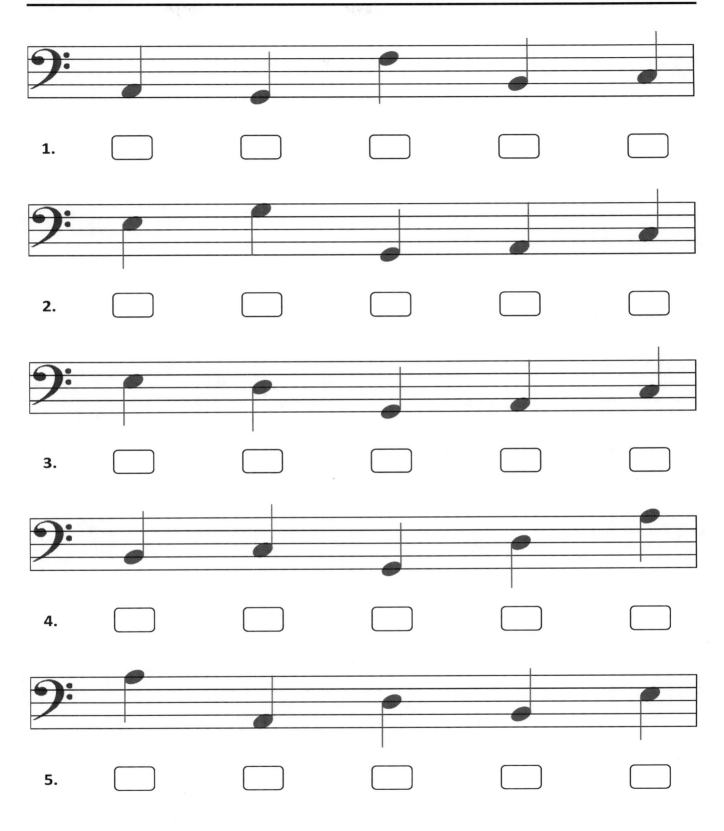

Completed On:_____   Number Correct:_____ / 25

1.

2.

3.

4.

5.

Completed On: _____   Number Correct: _____ / 25   Play me!

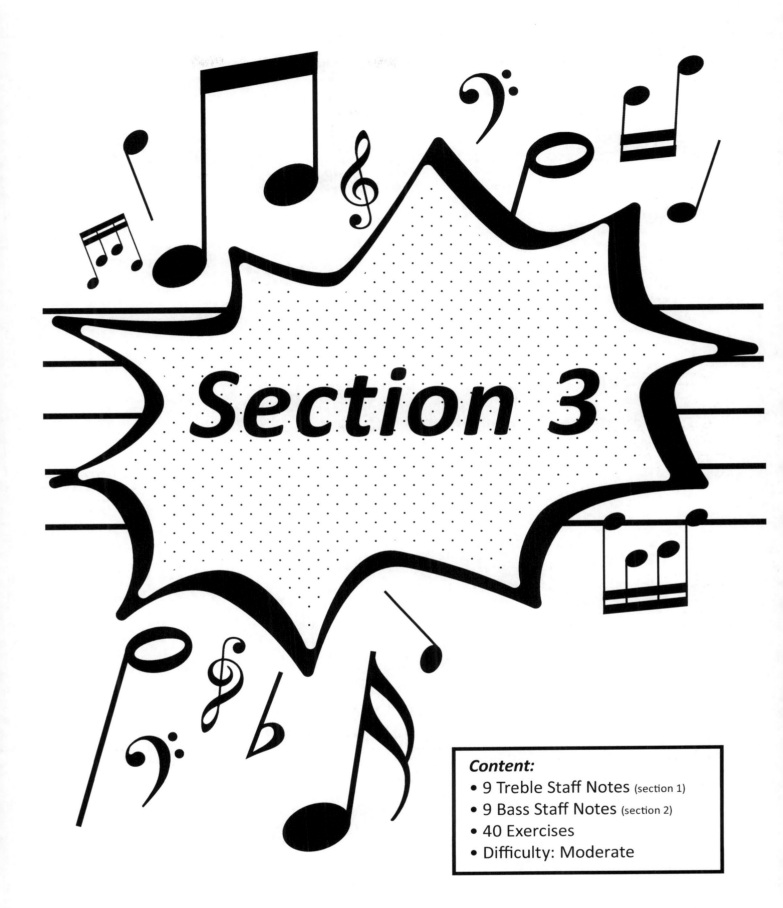

Section 3

Content:
- 9 Treble Staff Notes (section 1)
- 9 Bass Staff Notes (section 2)
- 40 Exercises
- Difficulty: Moderate

Notes Covered in Section 3

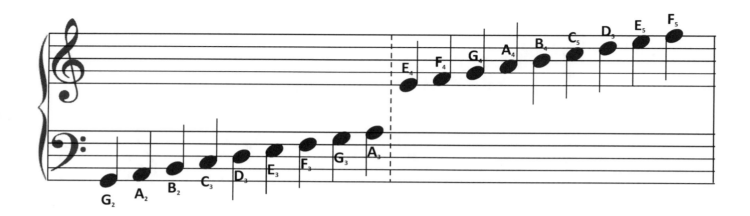

Instructions

1. Set a timer to one minute.
2. Label each note in the corresponding box.
3. After time expires, check your work with the Answer Key (pgs. 262-266).
4. Write the date and your score at the bottom of the page.

*If you finish in less than one minute, don't forget to check your work!
*If you do not complete all the notes in one minute, mark where you stopped and complete the unfinished as practice.

This graphic will appear at the bottom of every fifth page. After completing the exercises on these pages, play the notes on your instrument. Allow yourself one minute to play as many notes as possible.

Need Help? Check out the Note Reading Methods section on pages vii-viii.

Completed On: _____   Number Correct:_____ **/ 24**

1. ☐ ☐ ☐ ☐ ☐ ☐ ☐ ☐

2. ☐ ☐ ☐ ☐ ☐ ☐ ☐ ☐

3. ☐ ☐ ☐ ☐ ☐ ☐ ☐ ☐

Completed On: _____ **Number Correct:** _____ **/ 24**

Completed On: _____ **Number Correct:** _____ **/ 24**

1. ⬡ ⬡ ⬡ ⬡ ⬡ ⬡ ⬡ ⬡

2. ⬡ ⬡ ⬡ ⬡ ⬡ ⬡ ⬡ ⬡

3. ⬡ ⬡ ⬡ ⬡ ⬡ ⬡ ⬡ ⬡

Completed On: _____ **Number Correct:** _____ **/ 24**

1.

2.

3.

Completed On: _____   Number Correct: _____ / 24

Play me!

1. ▢ ▢ ▢ ▢ ▢ ▢ ▢ ▢

2. ▢ ▢ ▢ ▢ ▢ ▢ ▢ ▢

3. ▢ ▢ ▢ ▢ ▢ ▢ ▢ ▢

Completed On: _____ **Number Correct:** _____ **/ 24**

1.

2.

3.

Completed On: _____ Number Correct: _____ / 24

1. ☐ ☐ ☐ ☐ ☐ ☐ ☐ ☐

2. ☐ ☐ ☐ ☐ ☐ ☐ ☐ ☐

3. ☐ ☐ ☐ ☐ ☐ ☐ ☐ ☐

Play me!

Completed On: _____   Number Correct: _____ / 24

1. ☐ ☐ ☐ ☐ ☐ ☐ ☐ ☐

2. ☐ ☐ ☐ ☐ ☐ ☐ ☐ ☐

3. ☐ ☐ ☐ ☐ ☐ ☐ ☐ ☐

Completed On: _____   Number Correct: _____ / 24

1. ▢ ▢ ▢ ▢ ▢ ▢ ▢ ▢

2. ▢ ▢ ▢ ▢ ▢ ▢ ▢ ▢

3. ▢ ▢ ▢ ▢ ▢ ▢ ▢ ▢

Completed On: _____   **Number Correct:** _____ **/ 24**

Completed On: _____   Number Correct: _____ / 24

Completed On: _____

Number Correct: _____ **/ 24**

1.

2.

3.

Completed On:_____   Number Correct:_____ / 24

Completed On: _____

Number Correct: _____ / 24

Play me!

1. ☐ ☐ ☐ ☐ ☐ ☐ ☐ ☐

2. ☐ ☐ ☐ ☐ ☐ ☐ ☐ ☐

3. ☐ ☐ ☐ ☐ ☐ ☐ ☐ ☐

Completed On:_____   Number Correct:_____ / 24

1. ⬜ ⬜ ⬜ ⬜ ⬜ ⬜ ⬜ ⬜

2. ⬜ ⬜ ⬜ ⬜ ⬜ ⬜ ⬜ ⬜

3. ⬜ ⬜ ⬜ ⬜ ⬜ ⬜ ⬜ ⬜

Completed On: _____   **Number Correct:** _____ **/ 24**

1.

2.

3.

Completed On: _____   Number Correct: _____ / 24

Completed On:_____   Number Correct:_____ **/ 24**

1.

2.

3.

Completed On: _____   **Number Correct:** _____ **/ 24**

1.

2.

3.

Completed On: _____   **Number Correct:** _____ **/ 24**

1. ☐ ☐ ☐ ☐ ☐ ☐ ☐ ☐

2. ☐ ☐ ☐ ☐ ☐ ☐ ☐ ☐

3. ☐ ☐ ☐ ☐ ☐ ☐ ☐ ☐

Play me!

Completed On: _____   Number Correct: _____ / 24

Completed On: _____   Number Correct: _____ **/ 24**

1. ☐ ☐ ☐ ☐ ☐ ☐ ☐ ☐

2. ☐ ☐ ☐ ☐ ☐ ☐ ☐ ☐

3. ☐ ☐ ☐ ☐ ☐ ☐ ☐ ☐

Completed On: _____   **Number Correct:** _____ **/ 24**

1. ☐ ☐ ☐ ☐ ☐ ☐ ☐ ☐

2. ☐ ☐ ☐ ☐ ☐ ☐ ☐ ☐

3. ☐ ☐ ☐ ☐ ☐ ☐ ☐ ☐

Completed On: _____   **Number Correct:** _____ **/ 24**

Completed On: _____   Number Correct: _____ / 24

1.

2.

3.

Completed On:_____ Number Correct:_____ **/ 24**

1. ☐ ☐ ☐ ☐ ☐ ☐ ☐ ☐

2. ☐ ☐ ☐ ☐ ☐ ☐ ☐ ☐

3. ☐ ☐ ☐ ☐ ☐ ☐ ☐ ☐

Play me!

Completed On: _____   Number Correct: _____ / 24

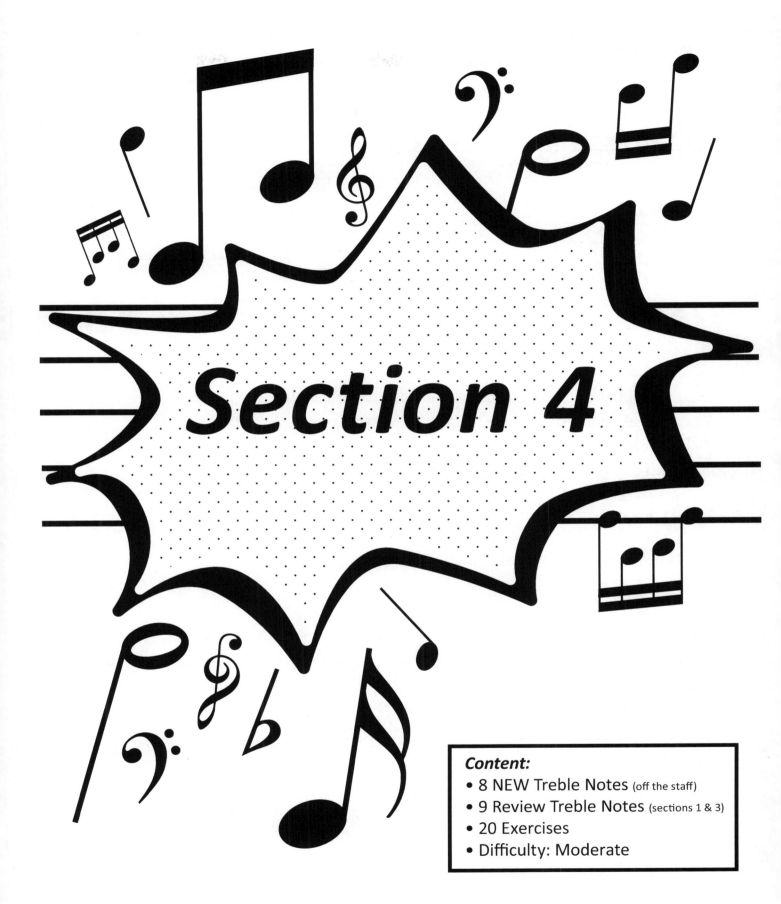

Section 4

Content:
- 8 NEW Treble Notes (off the staff)
- 9 Review Treble Notes (sections 1 & 3)
- 20 Exercises
- Difficulty: Moderate

Notes Covered in Section 4

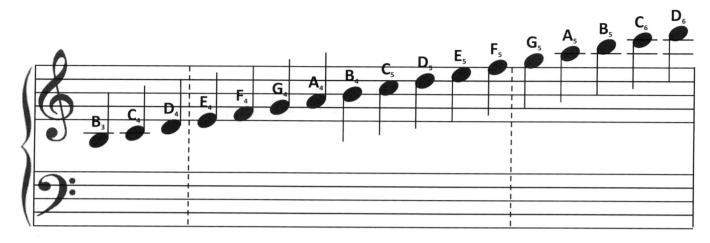

Instructions

1. Set a timer to one minute.
2. Label each note in the corresponding box.
3. After time expires, check your work with the Answer Key (pgs. 266-268).
4. Write the date and your score at the bottom of the page.

*If you finish in less than one minute, don't forget to check your work!
*If you do not complete all the notes in one minute, mark where you stopped and complete the unfinished as practice.

 This graphic will appear at the bottom of every fifth page. After completing the exercises on these pages, play the notes on your instrument. Allow yourself one minute to play as many notes as possible.

Need Help? Check out the Note Reading Methods section on pages vii-viii.

Completed On: _____   **Number Correct:** _____ **/ 25**

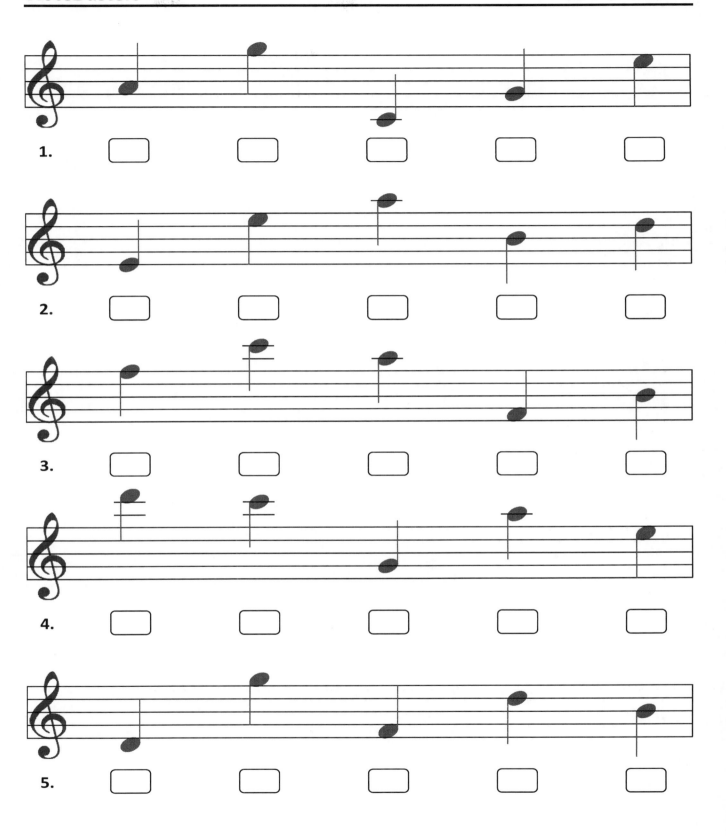

Completed On: _____   Number Correct: _____ **/ 25**

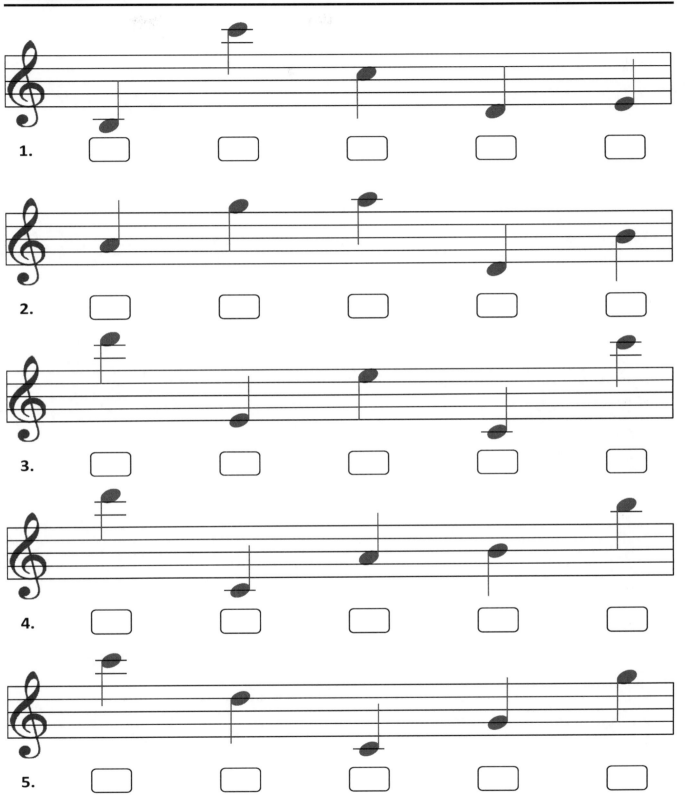

Completed On:_____   Number Correct:_____ / 25

Play me!

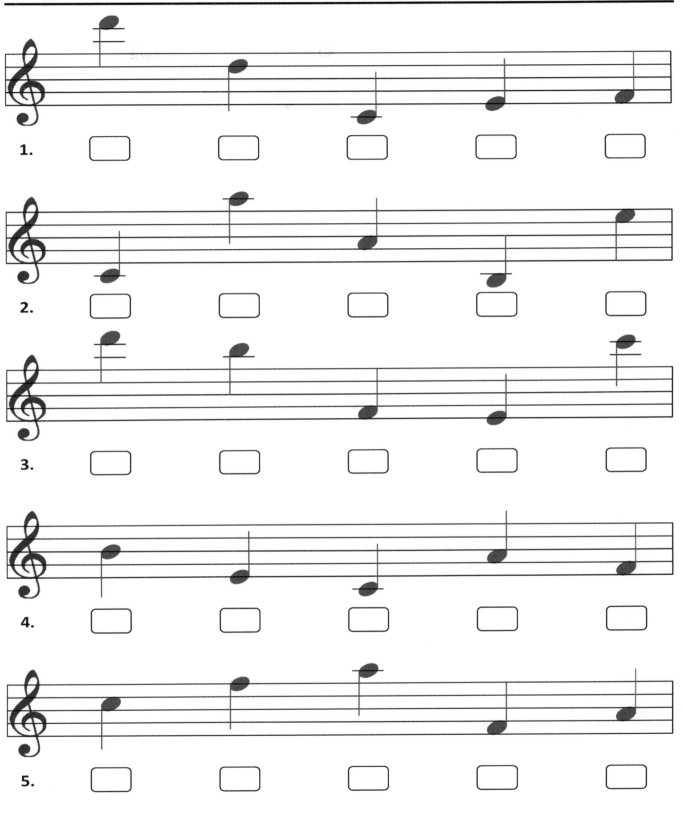

Completed On: _____   Number Correct: _____ / 25

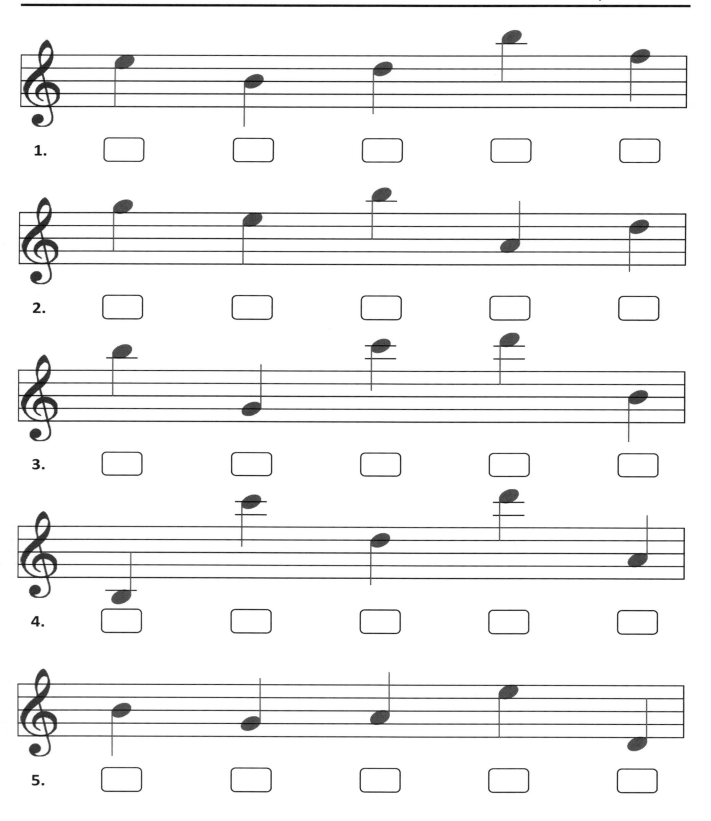

Completed On: _____   Number Correct: _____ / 25

Completed On: _____   **Number Correct:** _____ **/ 25**

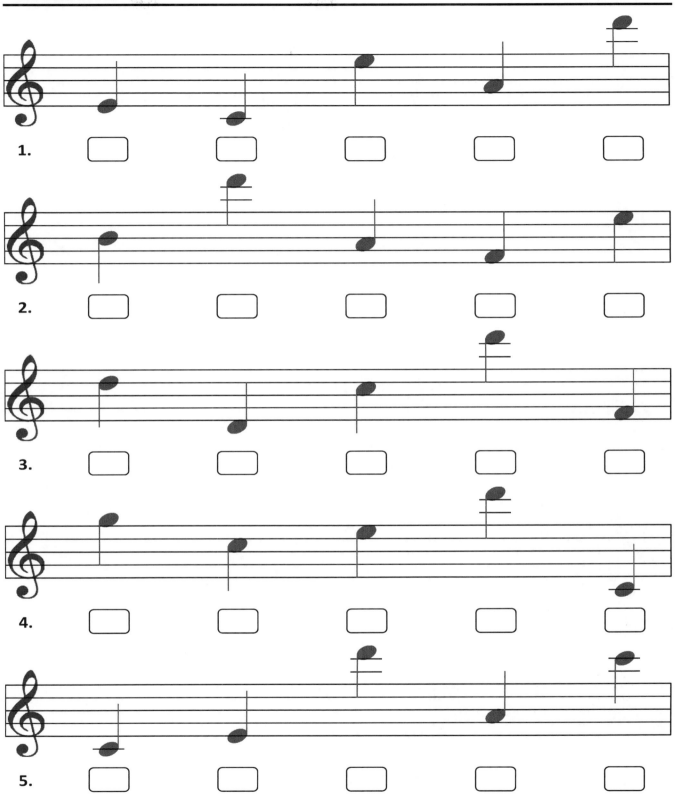

Completed On: _____   **Number Correct:** _____ **/ 25**

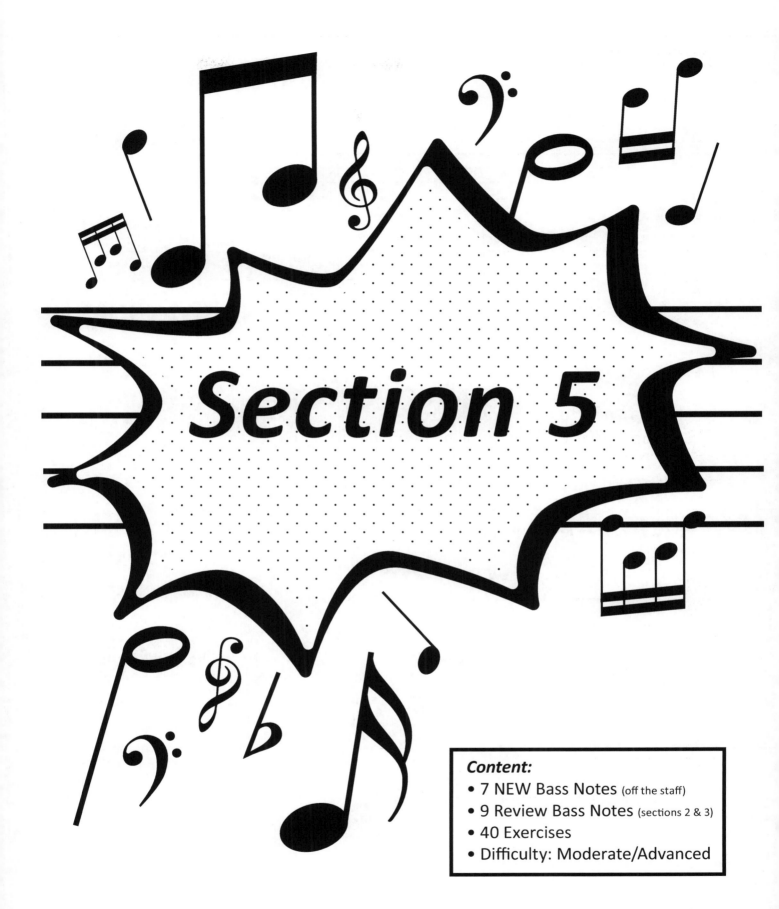

Section 5

Content:
- 7 NEW Bass Notes (off the staff)
- 9 Review Bass Notes (sections 2 & 3)
- 40 Exercises
- Difficulty: Moderate/Advanced

Notes Covered in Section 5

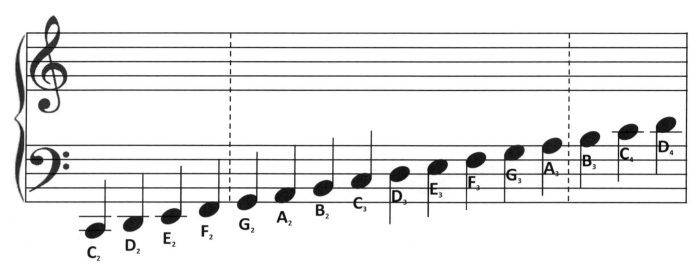

Instructions

1. Set a timer to one minute.
2. Label each note in the corresponding box.
3. After time expires, check your work with the Answer Key (pgs. 269-274).
4. Write the date and your score at the bottom of the page.

*If you finish in less than one minute, don't forget to check your work!
*If you do not complete all the notes in one minute, mark where you stopped and complete the unfinished as practice.

This graphic will appear at the bottom of every fifth page. After completing the exercises on these pages, play the notes on your instrument. Allow yourself one minute to play as many notes as possible.

Need Help? Check out the Note Reading Methods section on pages vii-viii.

Completed On: _____   **Number Correct:** _____ **/ 25**

Completed On: _____   **Number Correct:** _____ **/ 25**

Play me!

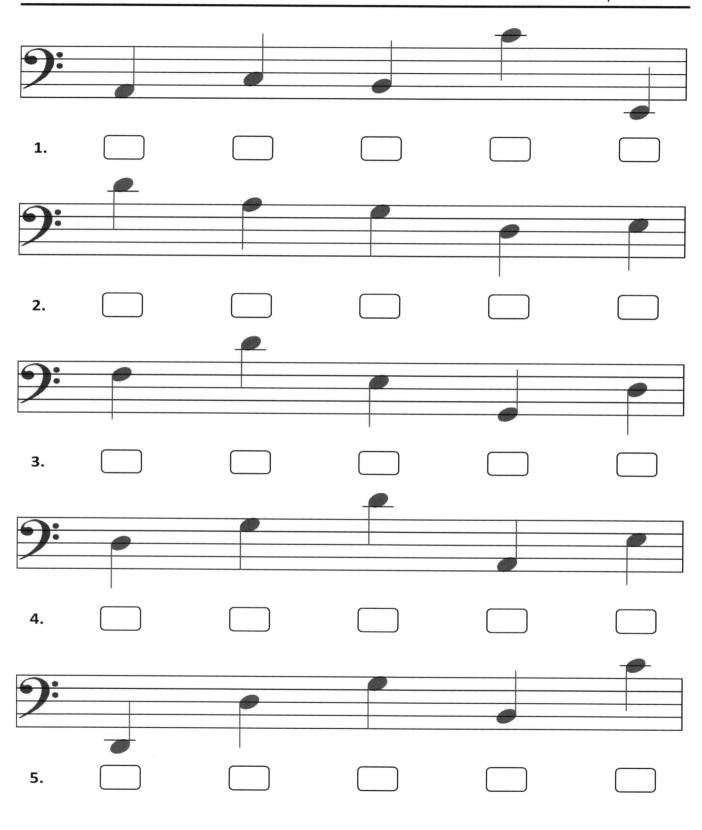

Completed On: _____   Number Correct: _____ / 25

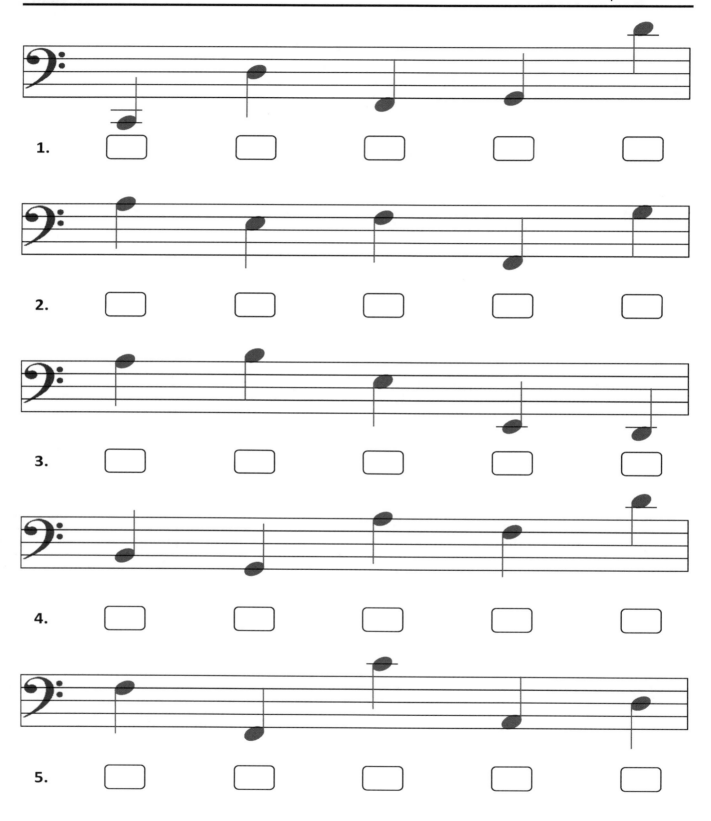

Completed On: _____   **Number Correct:** _____ **/ 25**

Play me!

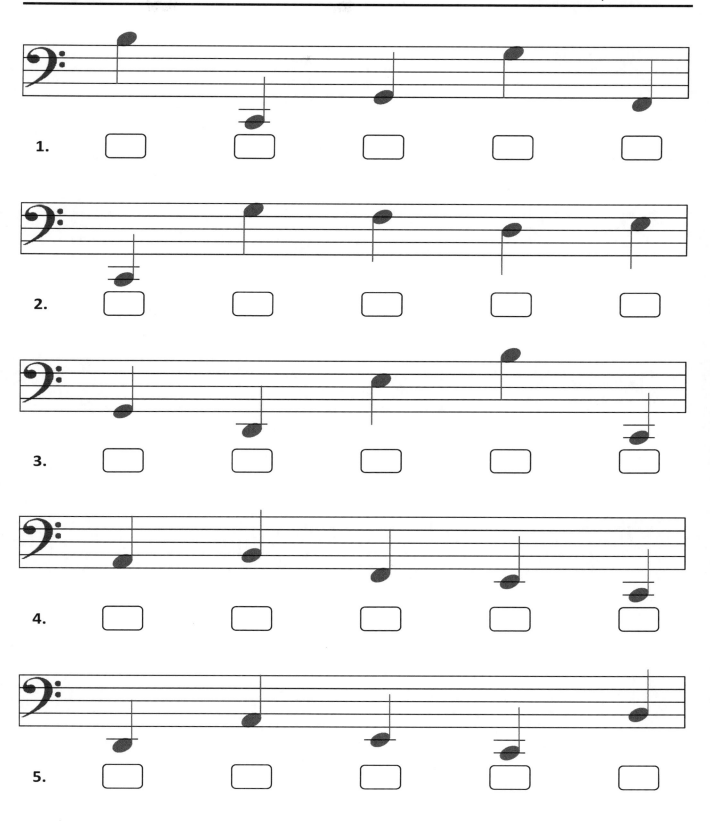

Completed On:_____   Number Correct:_____ / 25

1. ☐ ☐ ☐ ☐ ☐

2. ☐ ☐ ☐ ☐ ☐

3. ☐ ☐ ☐ ☐ ☐

4. ☐ ☐ ☐ ☐ ☐

5. ☐ ☐ ☐ ☐ ☐

Completed On: _____   **Number Correct:** _____ **/ 25**

Completed On: _____   Number Correct: _____ / 25

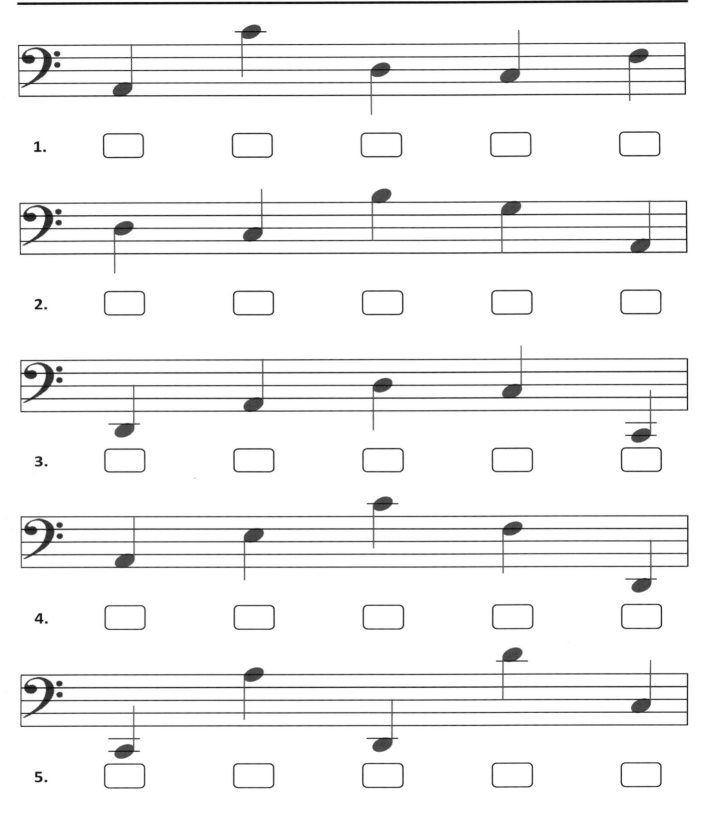

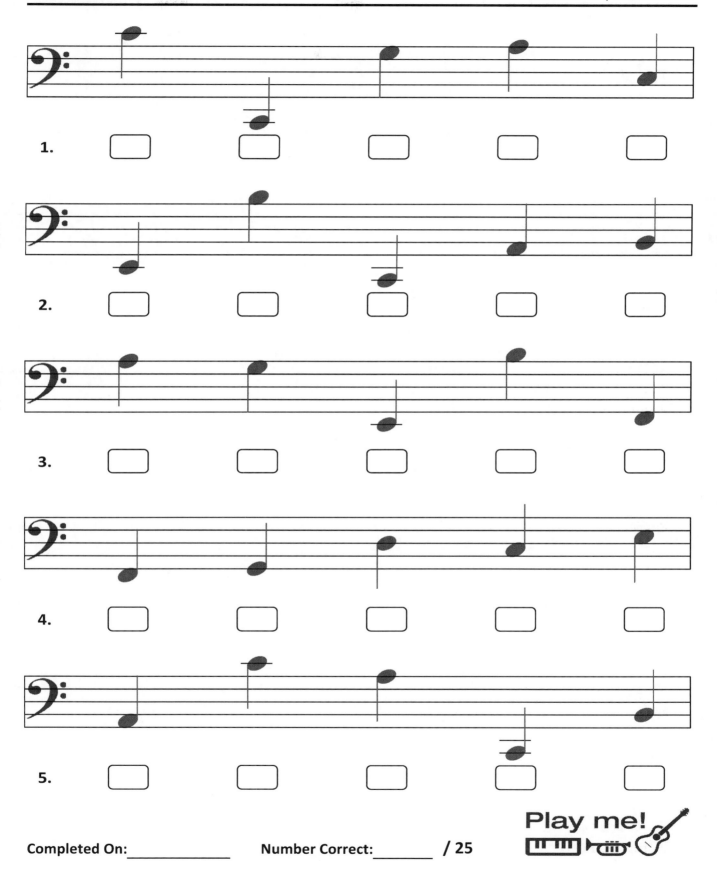

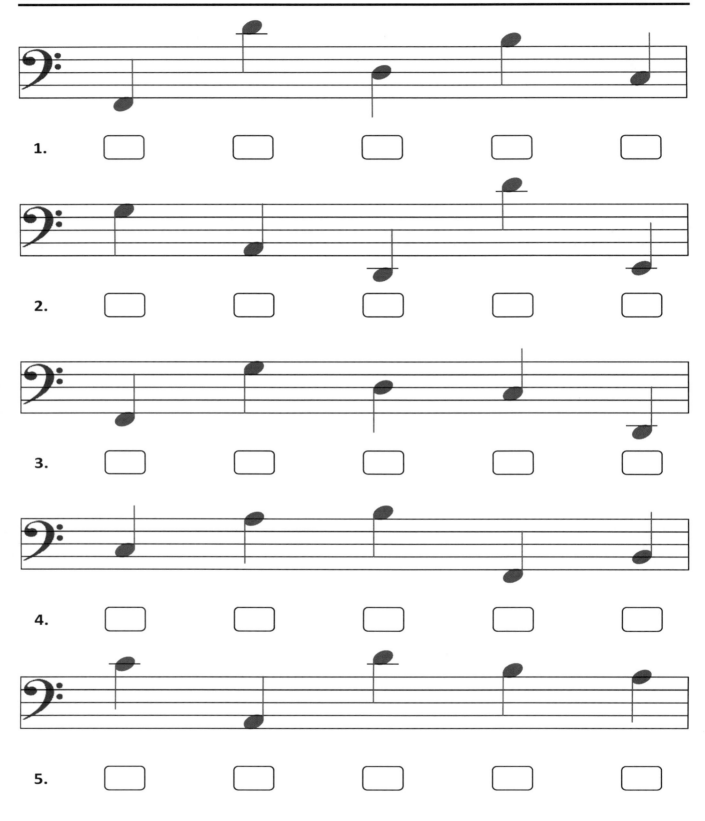

Completed On:_____   **Number Correct:**_____ **/ 25**

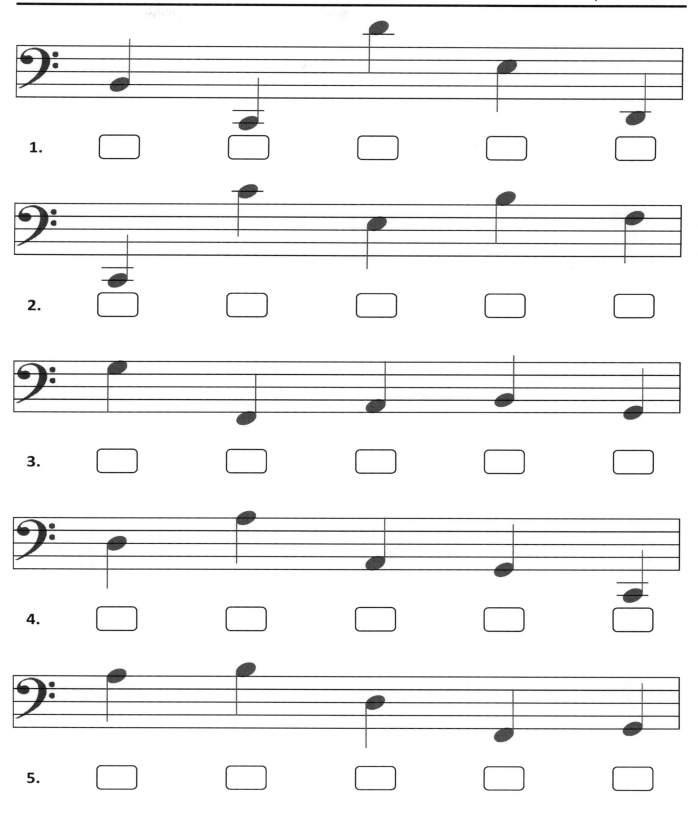

Completed On: _____

Number Correct: _____ / 25

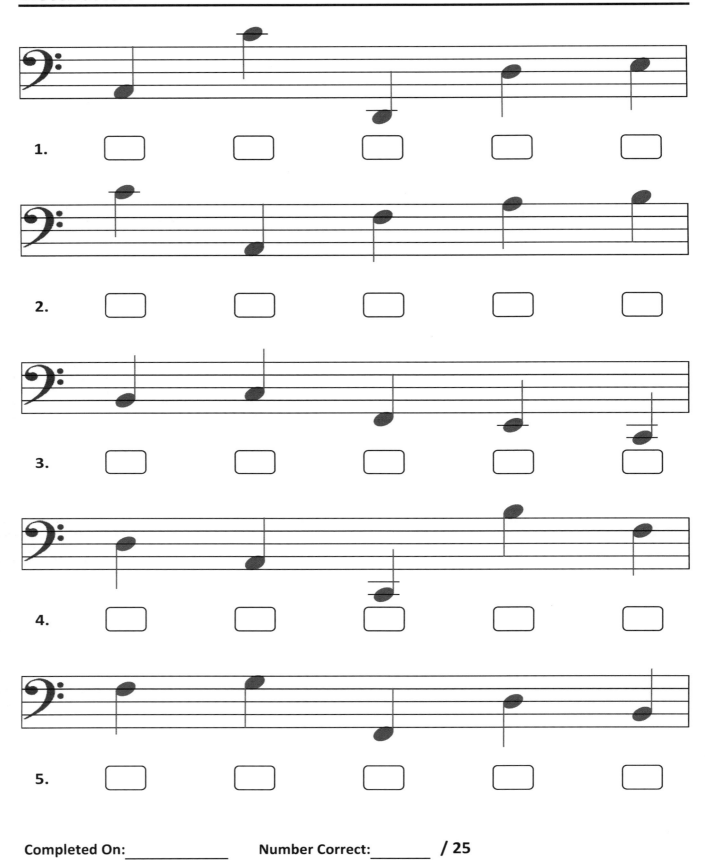

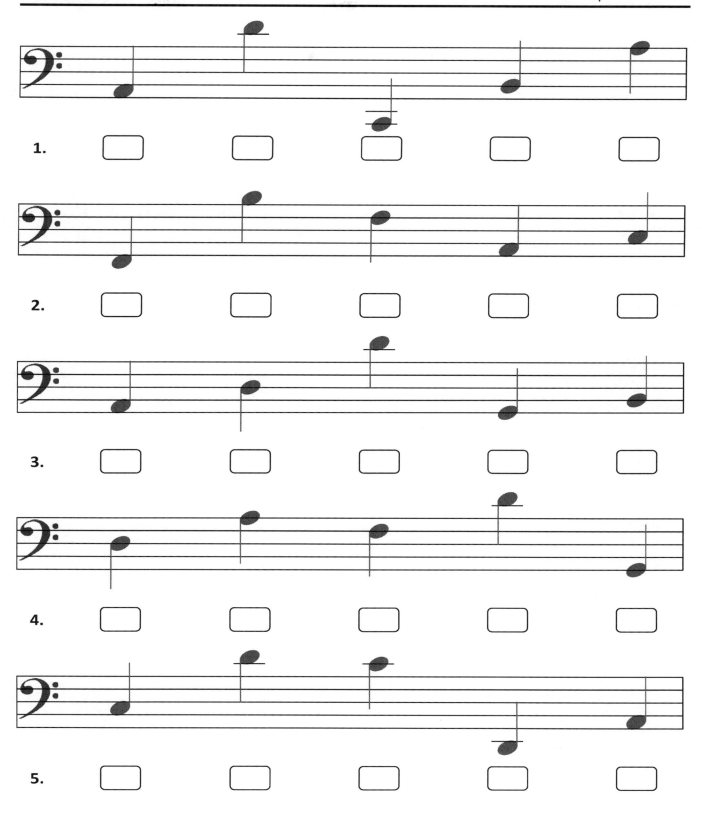

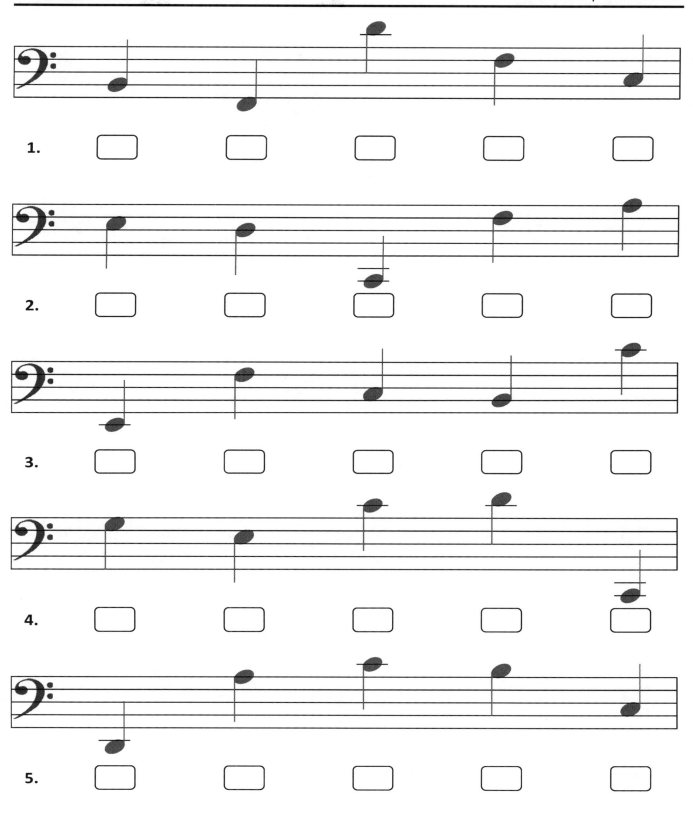

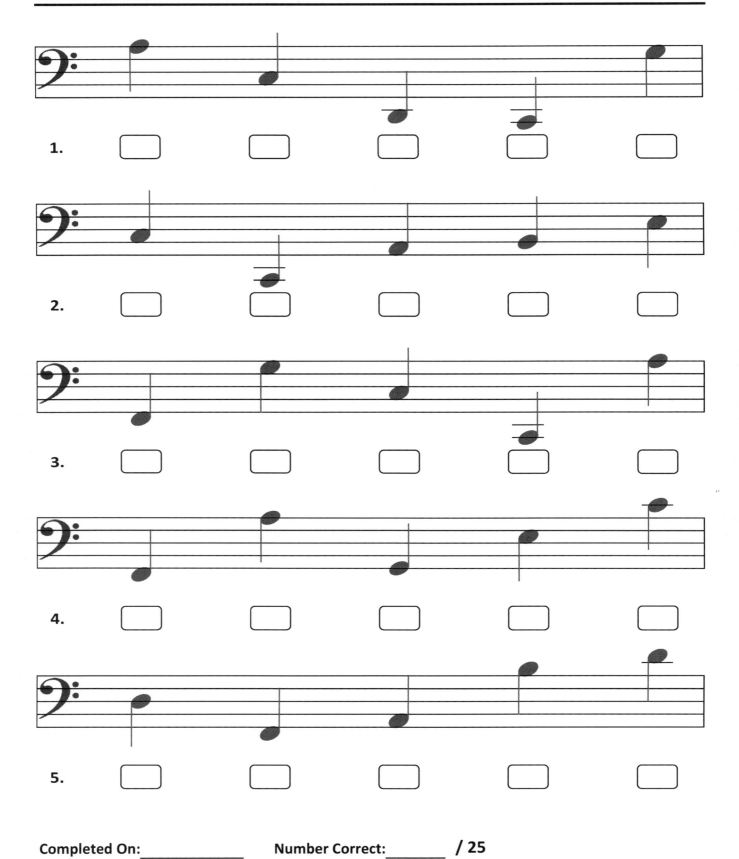

Completed On: _____   **Number Correct:** _____ **/ 25**

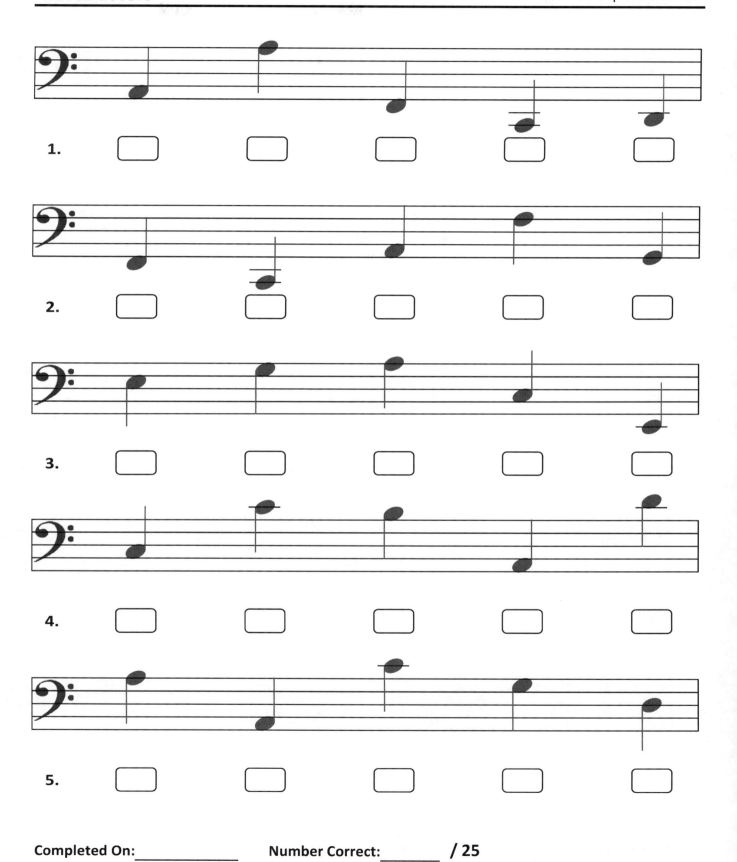

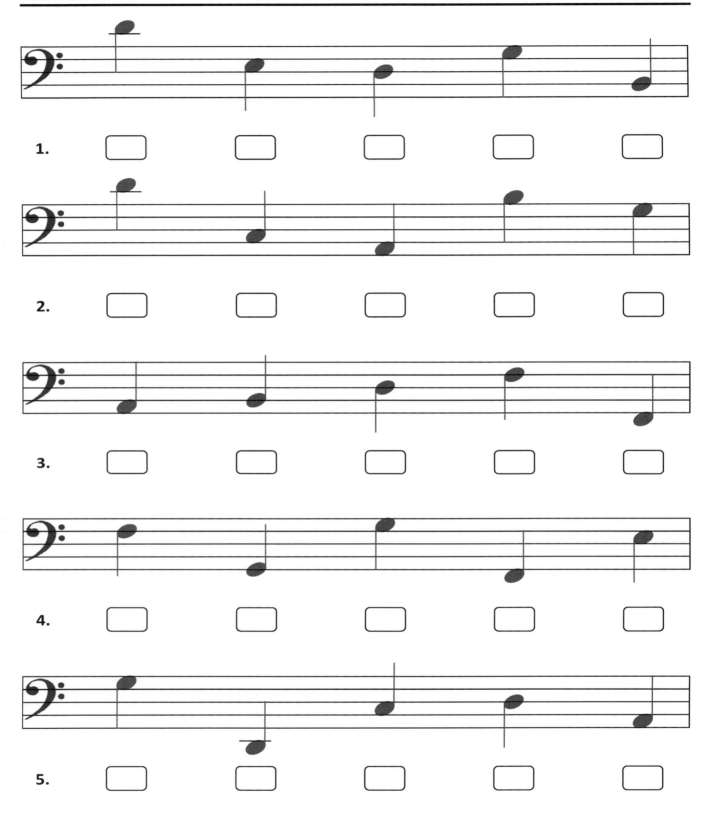

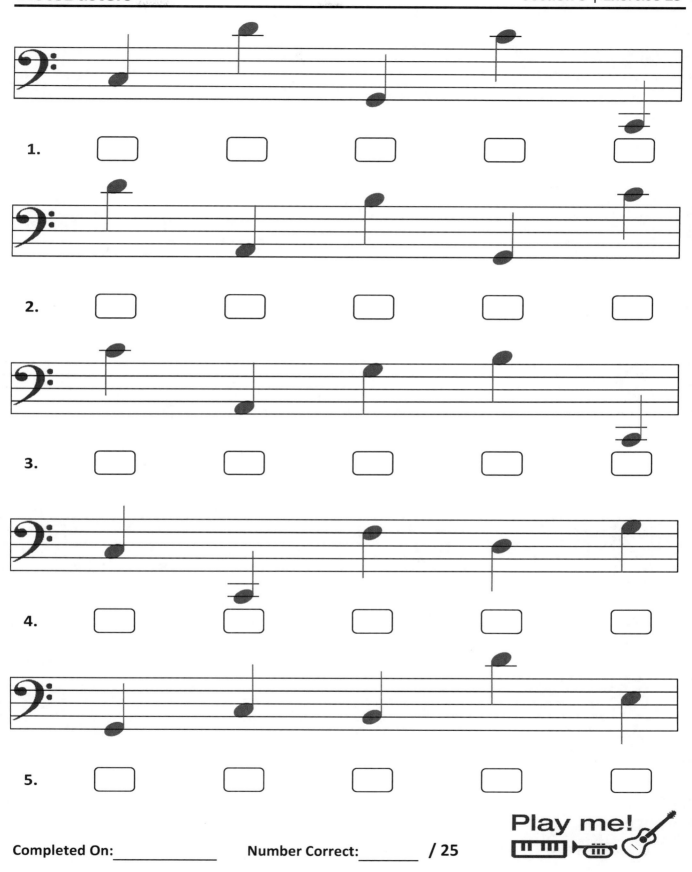

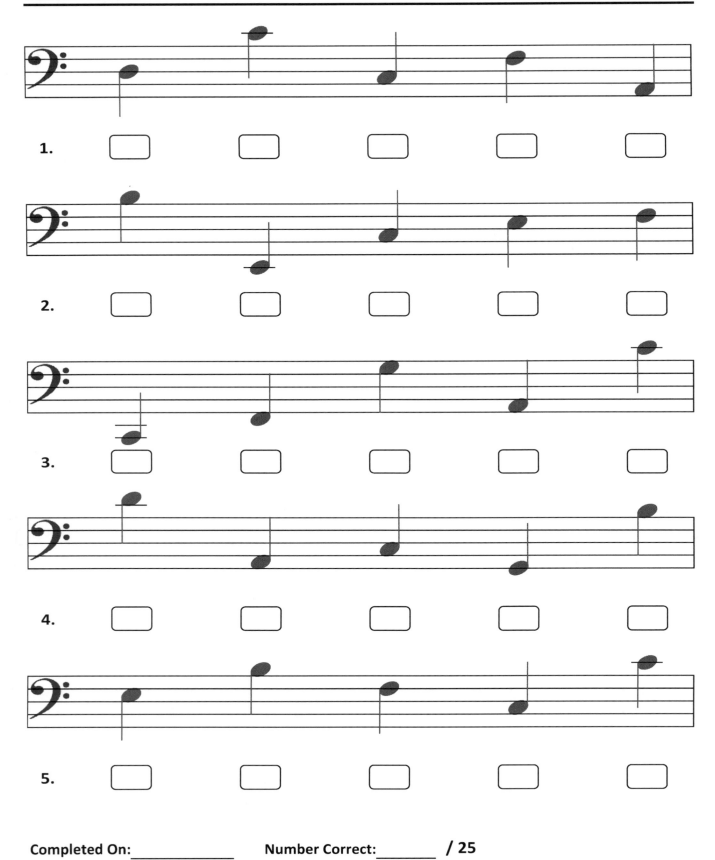

Completed On: _____ **Number Correct:** _____ **/ 25**

Completed On: _____   Number Correct: _____ / 25

Completed On: _____   **Number Correct:** _____ **/ 25**

1.

2.

3.

4.

5.

Completed On:_____   Number Correct:_____ / 25

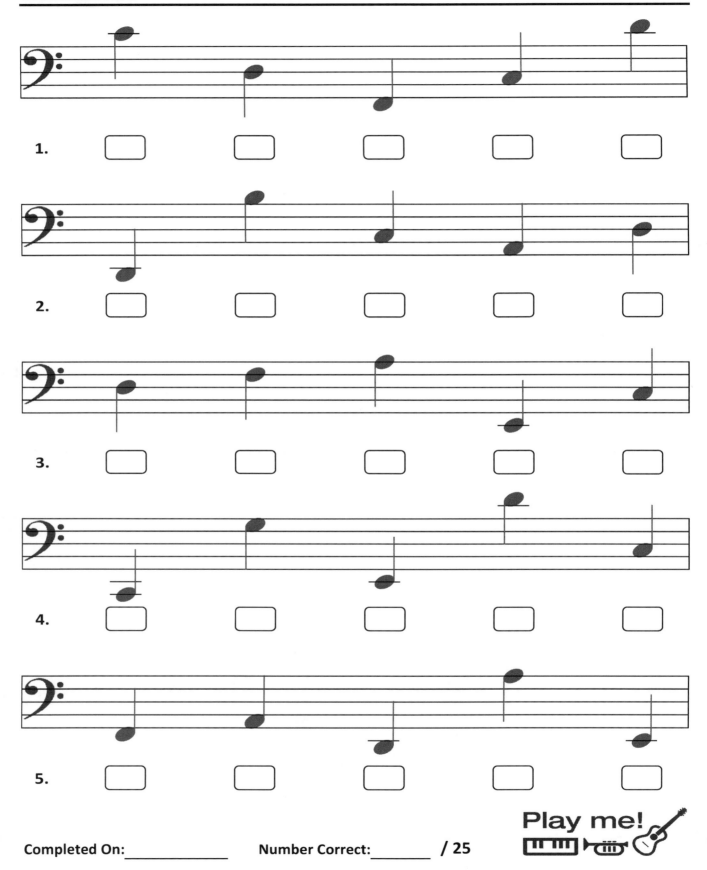

Completed On: _____   Number Correct: _____ / 25

Play me!

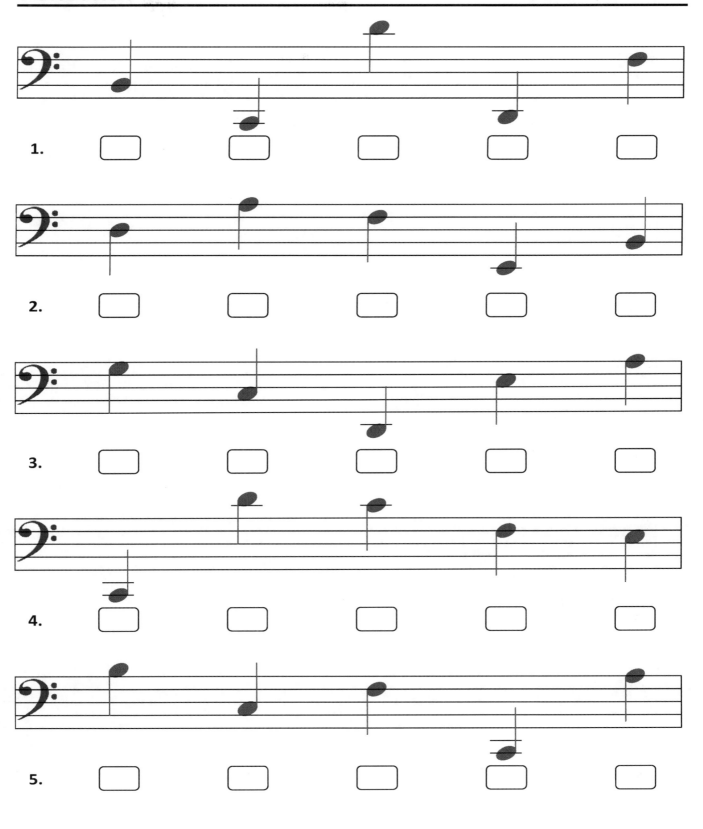

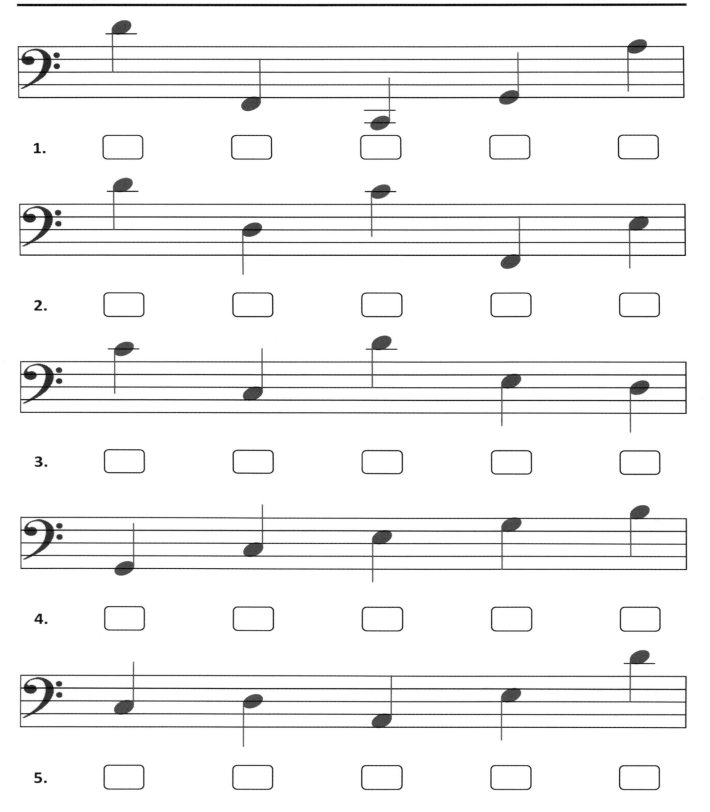

Completed On: _____   **Number Correct:** _____ **/ 25**

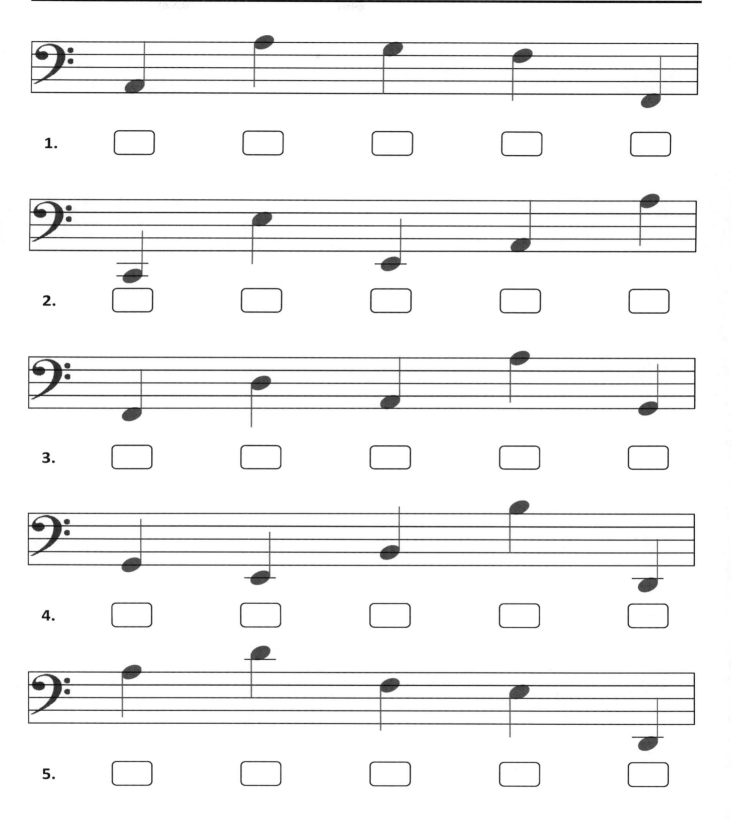

Completed On: _____   **Number Correct:** _____ **/ 25**

Completed On:_____   **Number Correct:**_____ **/ 25**

Completed On:_____   **Number Correct:**_____ / 25

Play me!

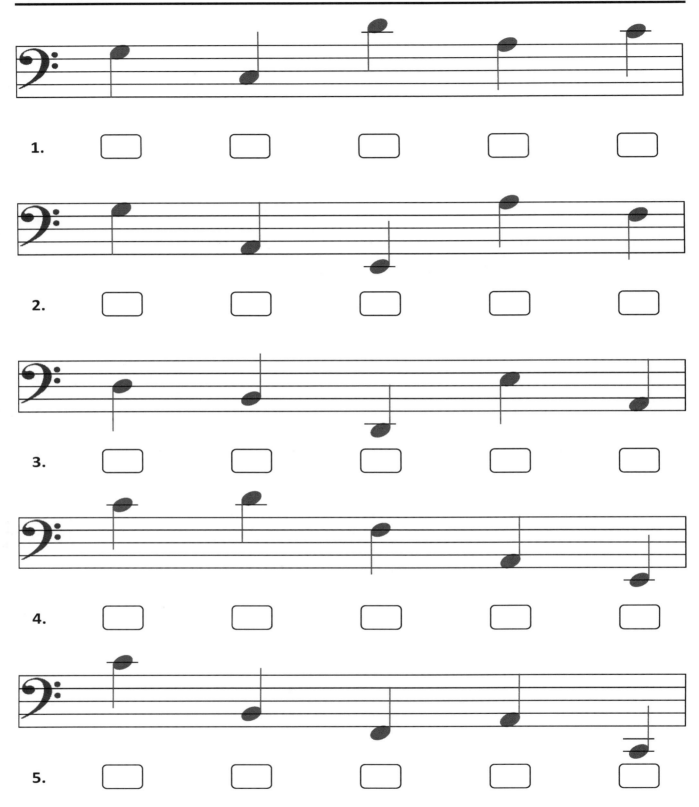

1. ☐ ☐ ☐ ☐ ☐

2. ☐ ☐ ☐ ☐ ☐

3. ☐ ☐ ☐ ☐ ☐

4. ☐ ☐ ☐ ☐ ☐

5. ☐ ☐ ☐ ☐ ☐

Completed On: _____   **Number Correct:** _____ **/ 25**

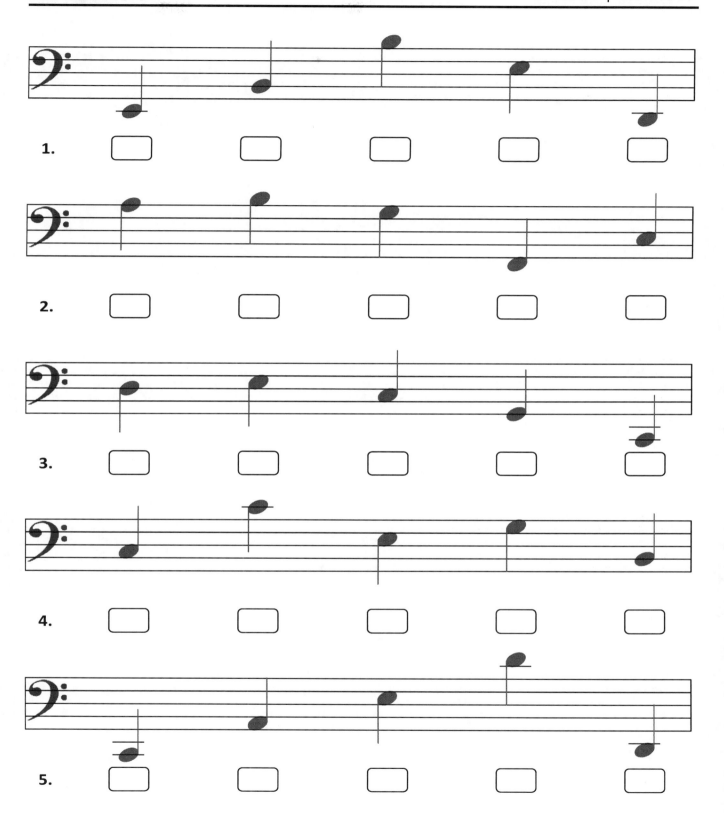

1.

2.

3.

4.

5.

Completed On:_____   Number Correct:_____ / 25

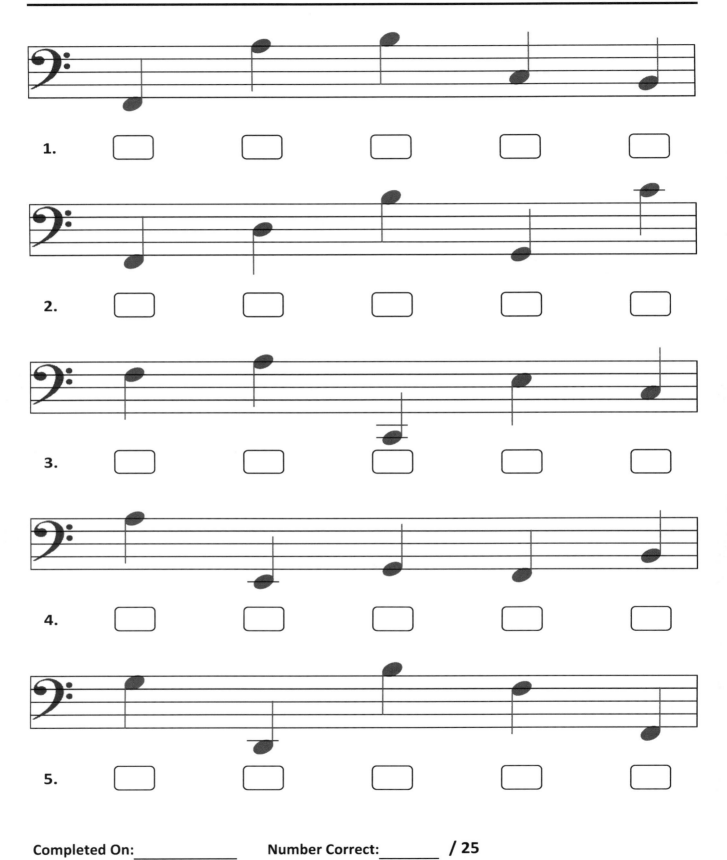

Completed On: _____   **Number Correct:** _____ **/ 25**

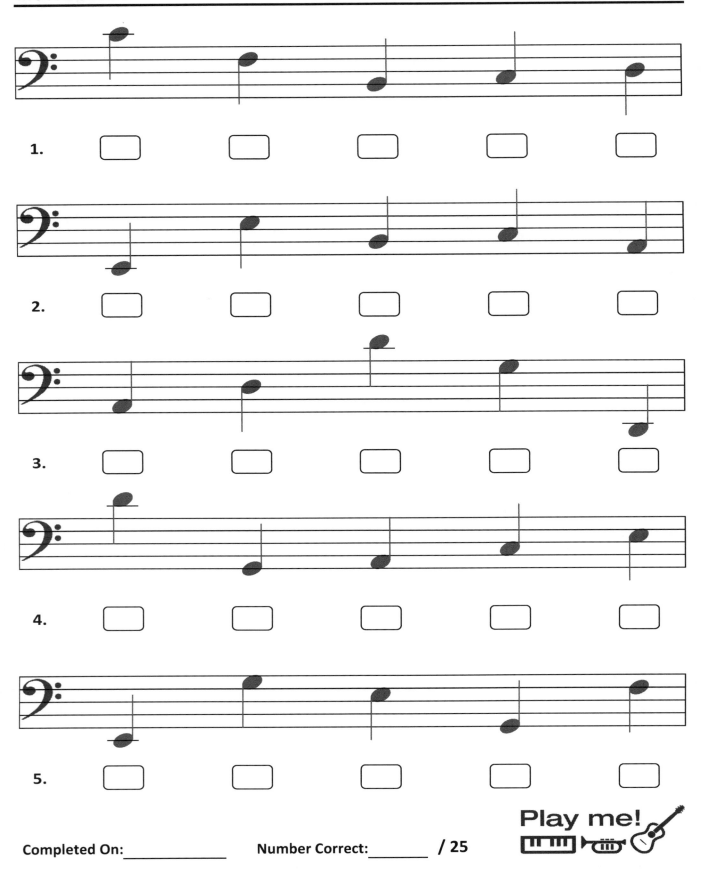

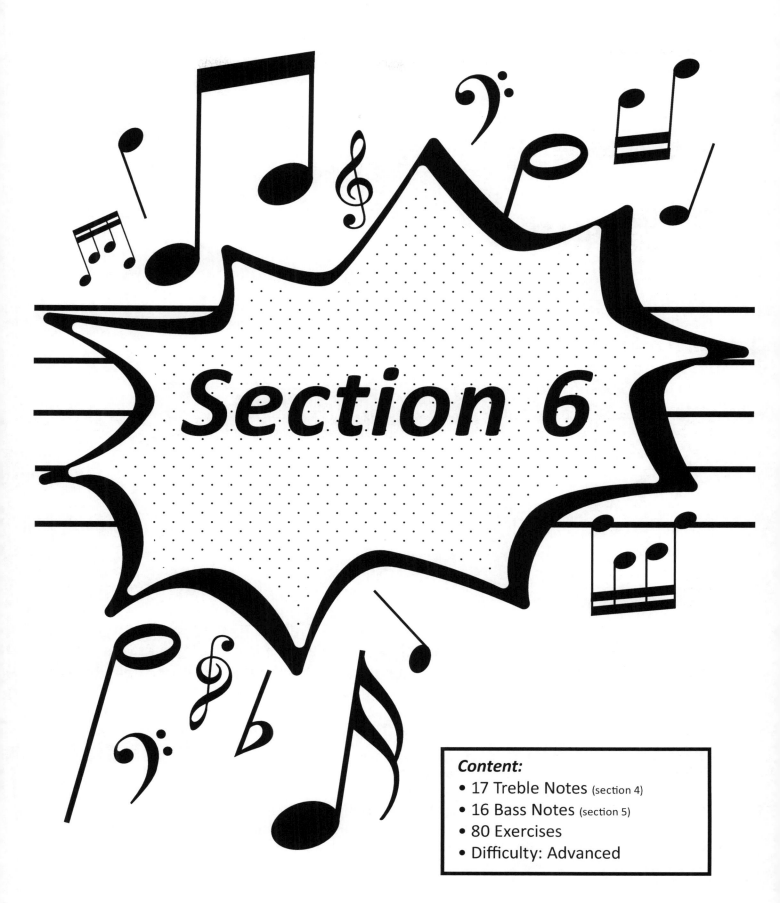

Content:
- 17 Treble Notes (section 4)
- 16 Bass Notes (section 5)
- 80 Exercises
- Difficulty: Advanced

Notes Covered in Section 6

Instructions

1. Set a timer to one minute.
2. Label each note in the corresponding box.
3. After time expires, check your work with the Answer Key (pgs.274-281).
4. Write the date and your score at the bottom of the page.

*If you finish in less than one minute, don't forget to check your work!
*If you do not complete all the notes in one minute, mark where you stopped and complete the unfinished as practice.

This graphic will appear at the bottom of every fifth page. After completing the exercises on these pages, play the notes on your instrument. Allow yourself one minute to play as many notes as possible.

Need Help? Check out the Note Reading Methods section on pages vii-viii.

This is the final section in the workbook. After completing this section you will have mastered over 30 notes on both the treble and bass staves! If you are interested in additional exercises from any of the sections contained in this book, please contact the publisher at general@notebusters.net

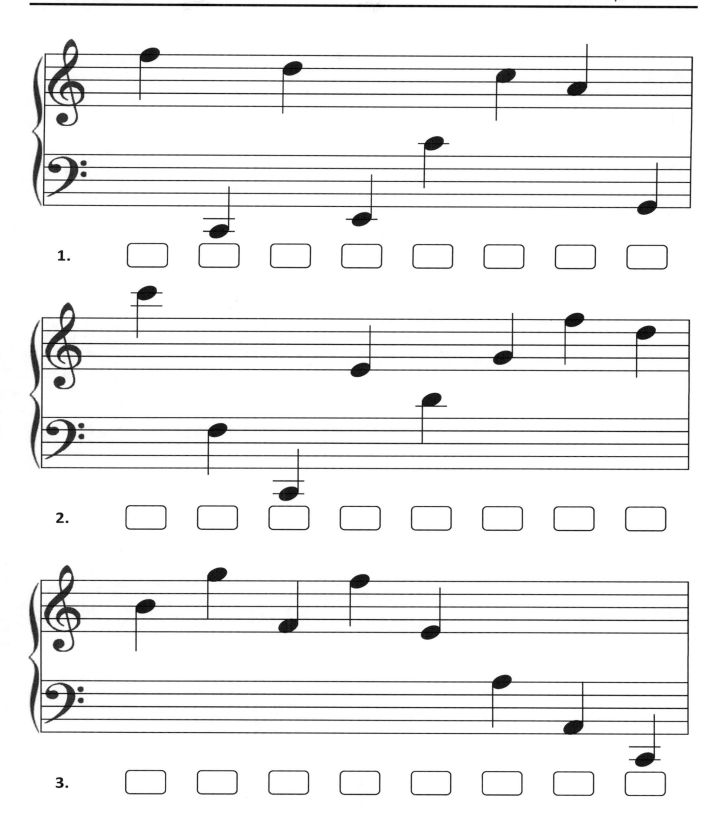

1.

2.

3.

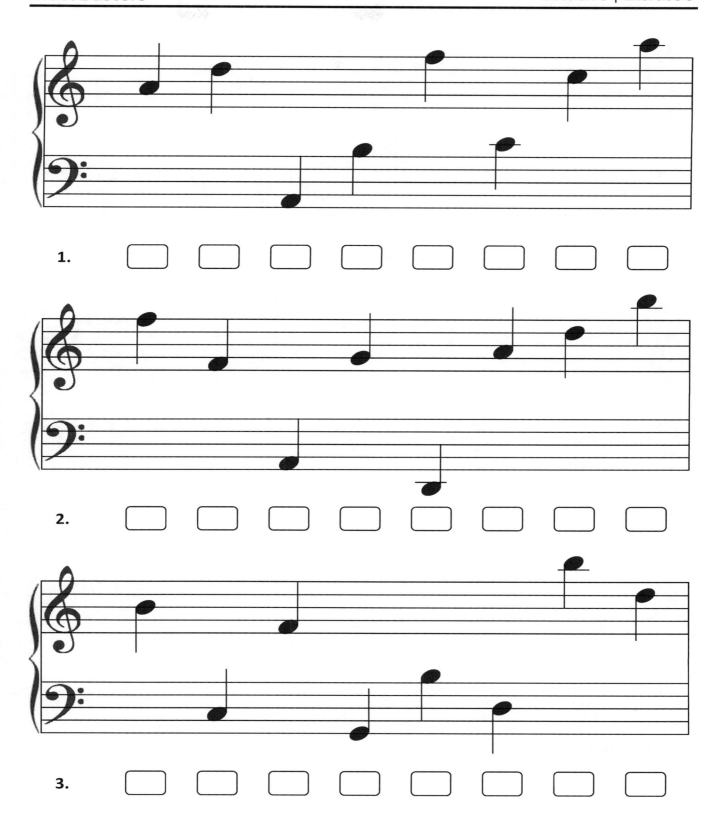

1.

2.

3.

Completed On: _____   Number Correct: _____ / 24

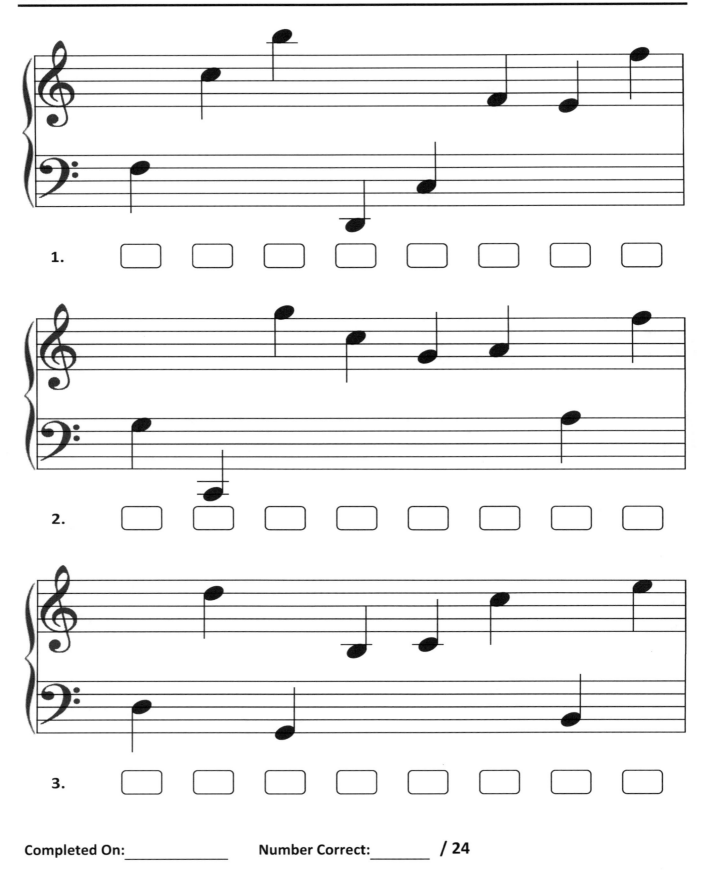

Completed On: _____   Number Correct: _____ / 24

1.

2.

3.

Completed On: _____   Number Correct: _____ / 24   Play me!

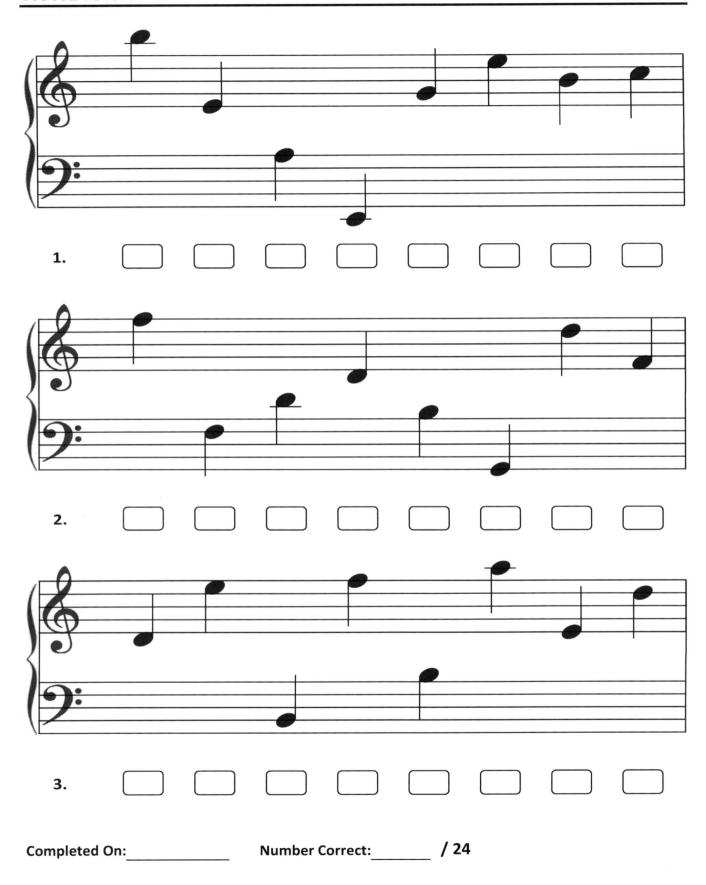

1. ☐ ☐ ☐ ☐ ☐ ☐ ☐ ☐

2. ☐ ☐ ☐ ☐ ☐ ☐ ☐ ☐

3. ☐ ☐ ☐ ☐ ☐ ☐ ☐ ☐

Completed On: _____   **Number Correct:** _____ **/ 24**

1. ☐ ☐ ☐ ☐ ☐ ☐ ☐ ☐

2. ☐ ☐ ☐ ☐ ☐ ☐ ☐ ☐

3. ☐ ☐ ☐ ☐ ☐ ☐ ☐ ☐

Completed On: _____   Number Correct:_____ / 24

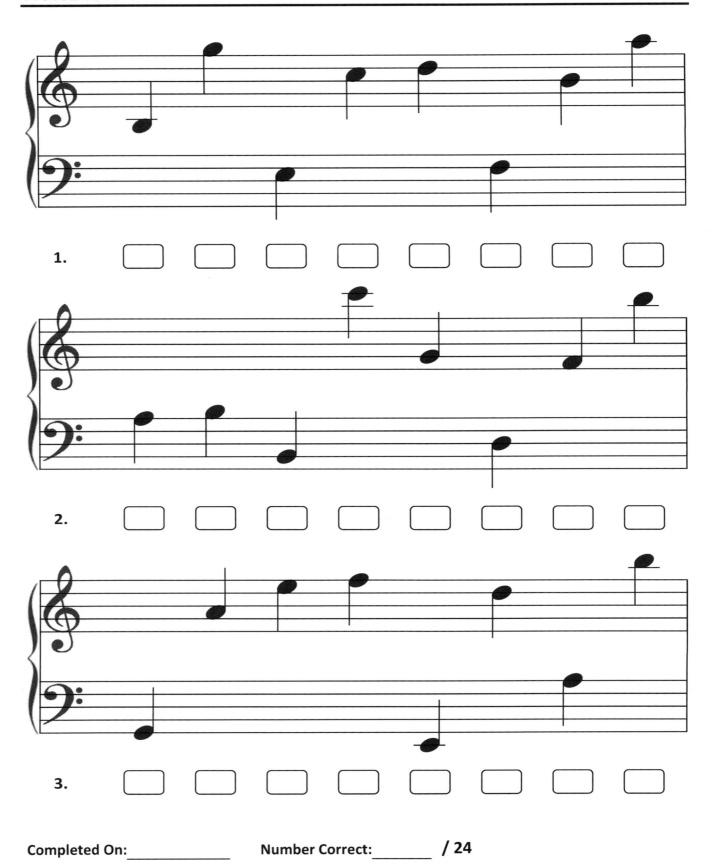

1. ☐ ☐ ☐ ☐ ☐ ☐ ☐ ☐

2. ☐ ☐ ☐ ☐ ☐ ☐ ☐ ☐

3. ☐ ☐ ☐ ☐ ☐ ☐ ☐ ☐

Completed On: _____   Number Correct: _____ / 24

1.

2.

3.

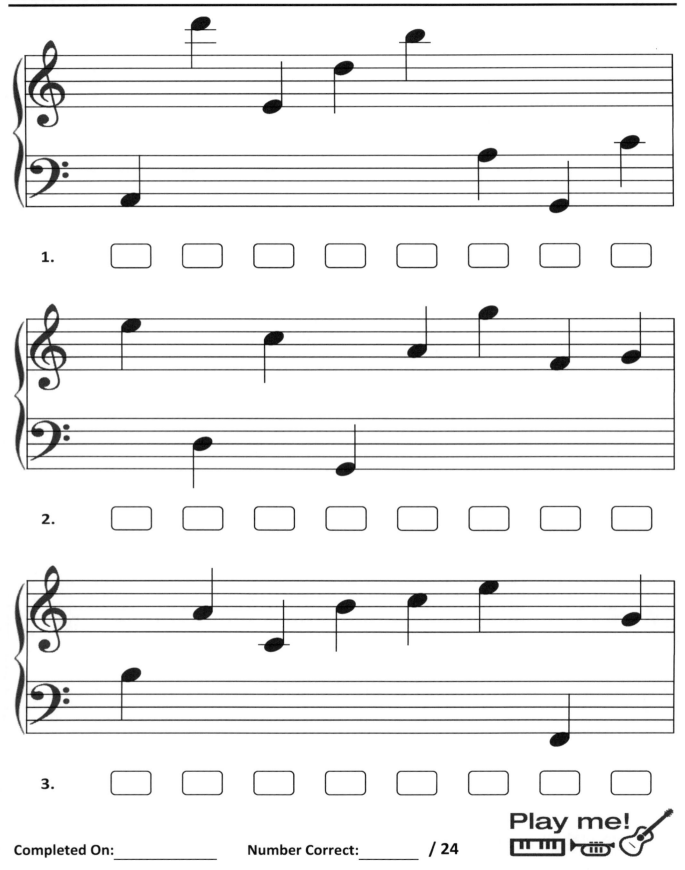

Completed On:_____   Number Correct:_____ / 24

Play me!

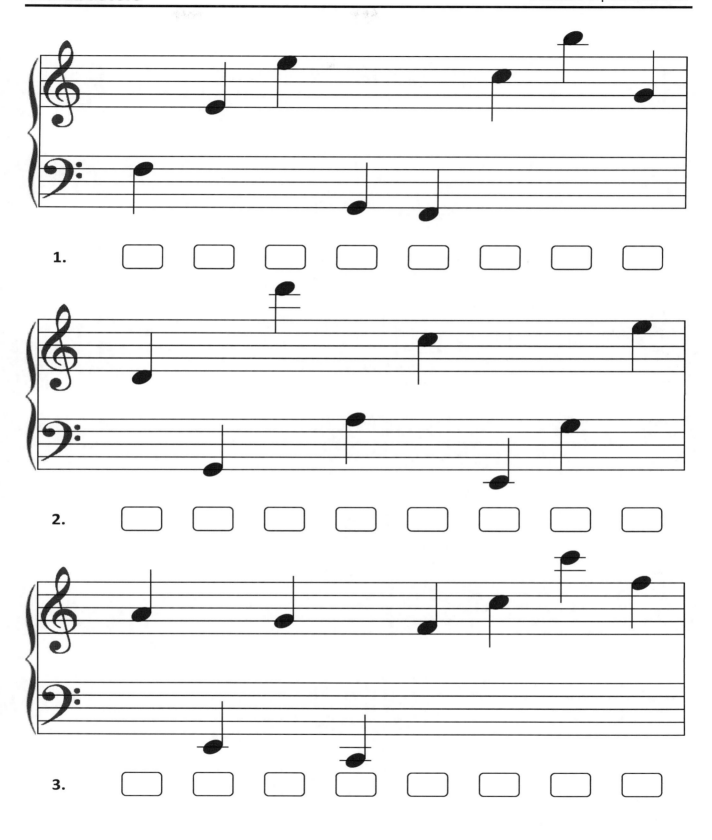

1.

2.

3.

Completed On:_____   Number Correct:_____ / 24

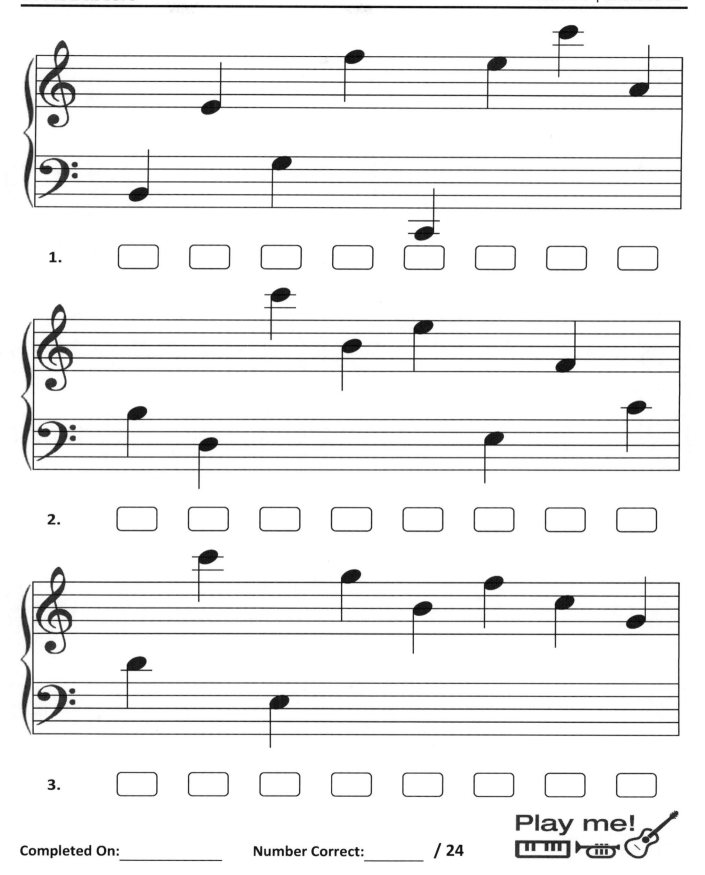

Play me!

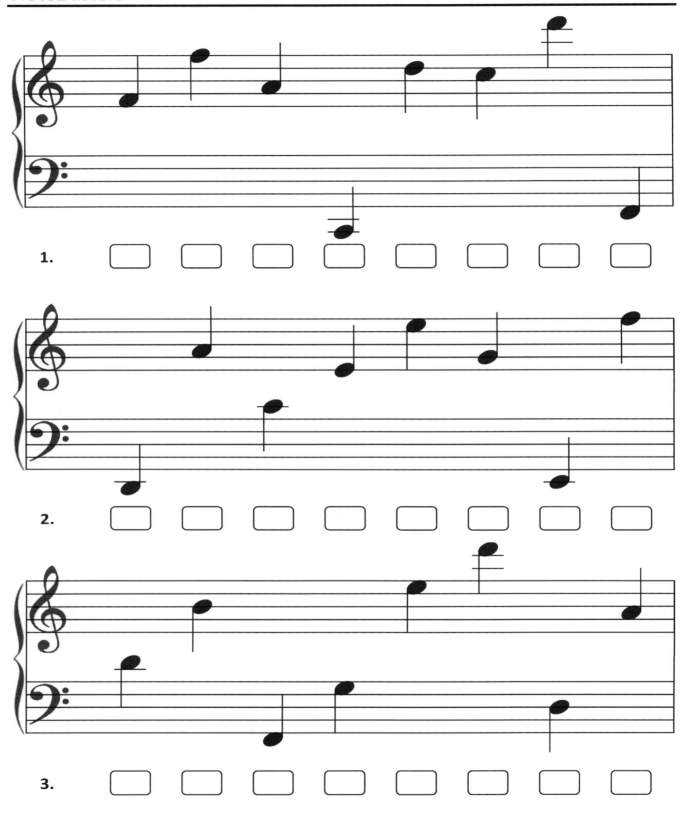

1.

2.

3.

1.

2.

3.

Completed On: _____   **Number Correct:** _____ **/ 24**

1.

2.

3.

Completed On: _____   **Number Correct:** _____ **/ 24**

1.

2.

3.

Completed On: _____   Number Correct: _____ / 24

Play me!

1.

2.

3.

Completed On: _____   Number Correct: _____ / 24

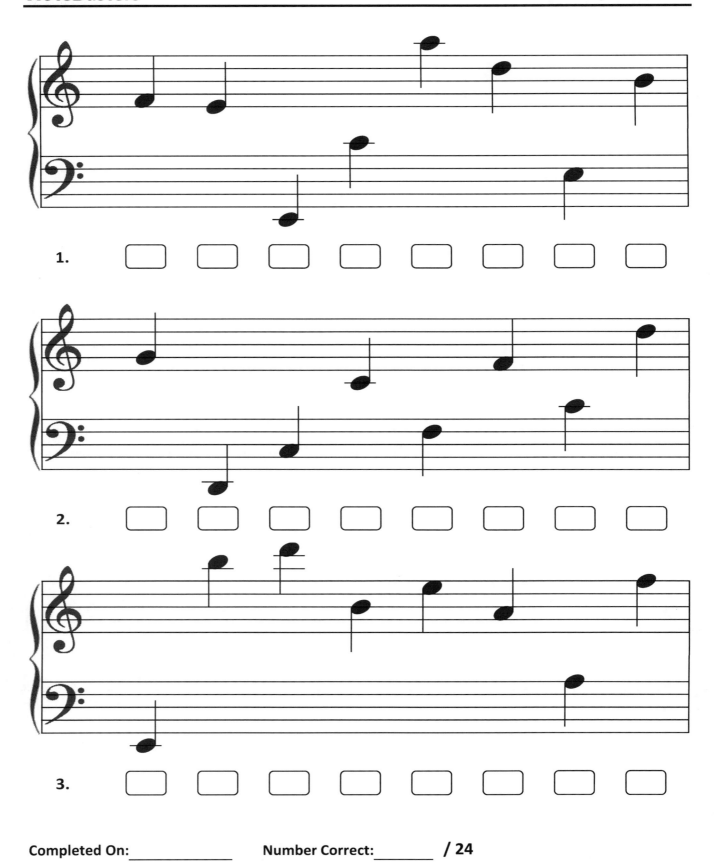

Completed On: _____   Number Correct: _____ / 24

Completed On: _____   Number Correct: _____ / 24

1.

2.

3.

Completed On:_____   Number Correct:_____ / 24

1.

2.

3.

Completed On: _____ Number Correct: _____ / 24

Play me!

1.

2.

3.

Completed On: _____   Number Correct: _____ / 24

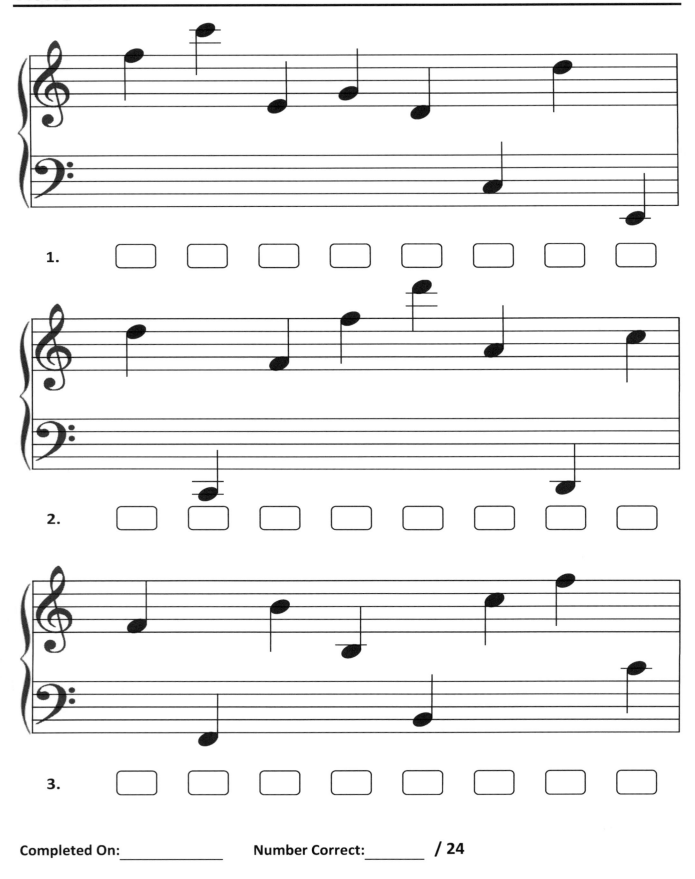

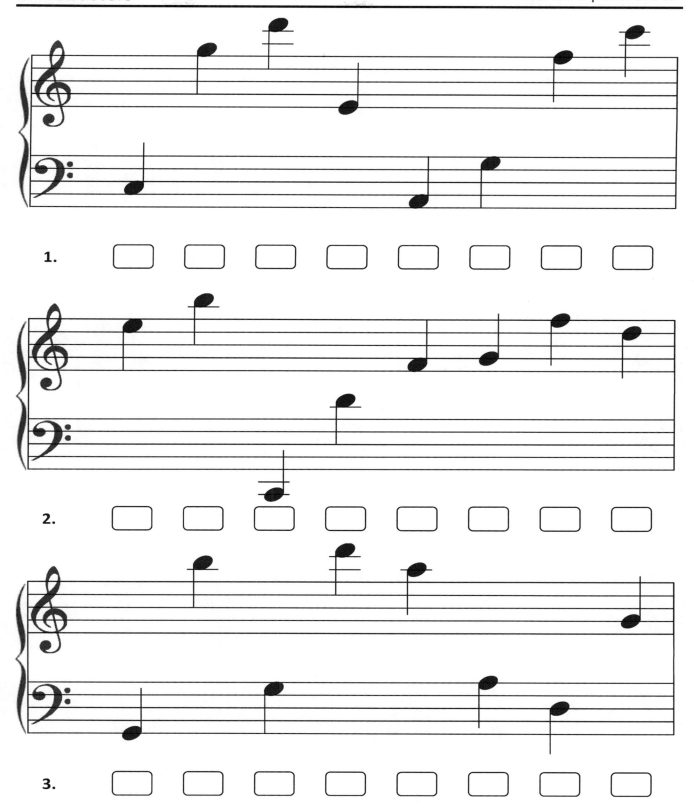

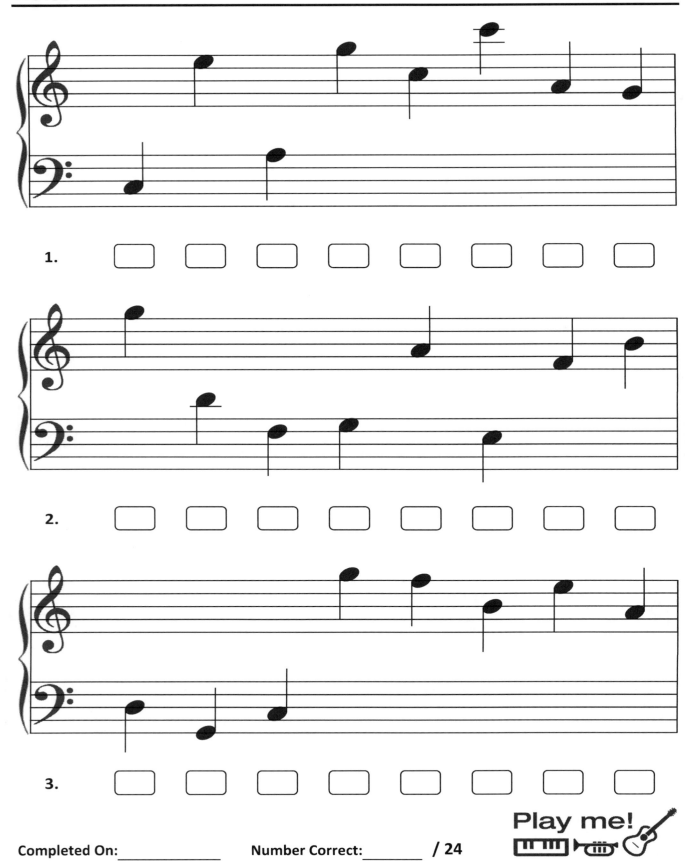

1. ☐ ☐ ☐ ☐ ☐ ☐ ☐ ☐

2. ☐ ☐ ☐ ☐ ☐ ☐ ☐ ☐

3. ☐ ☐ ☐ ☐ ☐ ☐ ☐ ☐

Play me!

Completed On: _____　　Number Correct: _____ / 24

1.

2.

3.

Completed On: _____   Number Correct: _____ / 24

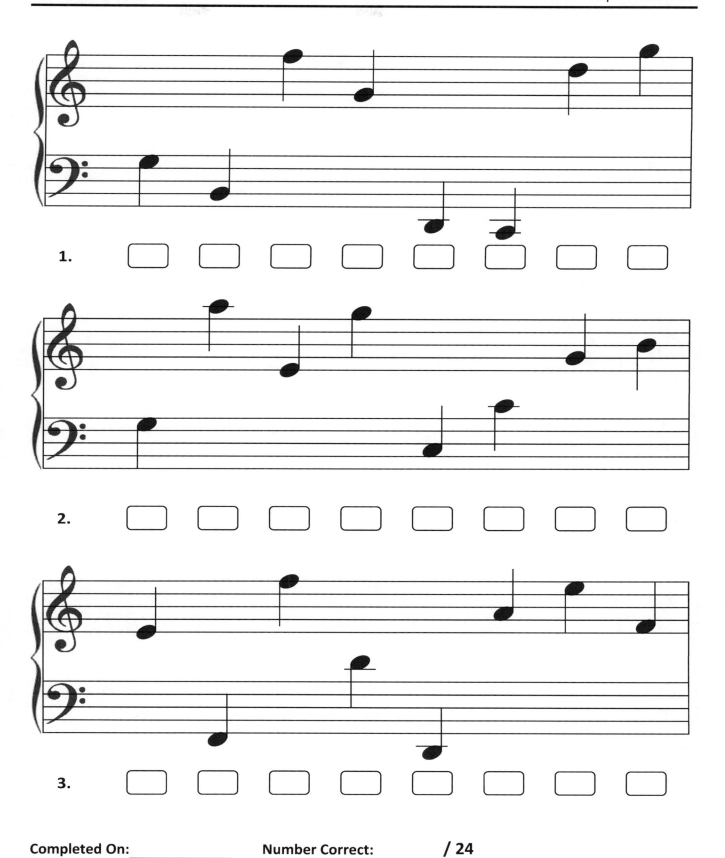

Completed On:_____ **Number Correct:**_____ **/ 24**

1. ☐ ☐ ☐ ☐ ☐ ☐ ☐ ☐

2. ☐ ☐ ☐ ☐ ☐ ☐ ☐ ☐

3. ☐ ☐ ☐ ☐ ☐ ☐ ☐ ☐

Completed On:_____   Number Correct:_____ / 24

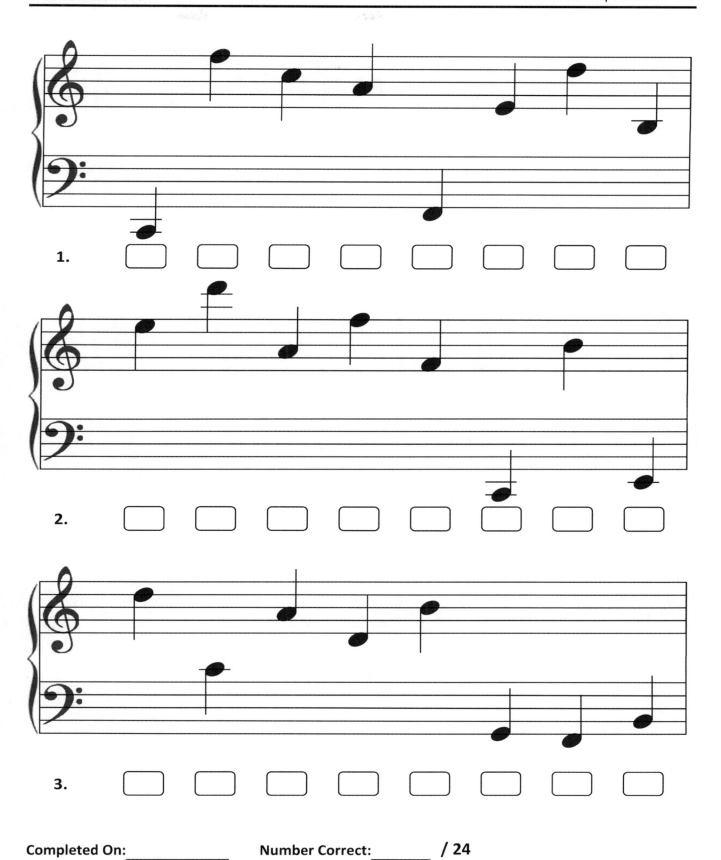

1.

2.

3.

Completed On: _____ **Number Correct:** _____ / 24

1.

2.

3.

Completed On: _____   Number Correct: _____ **/ 24**

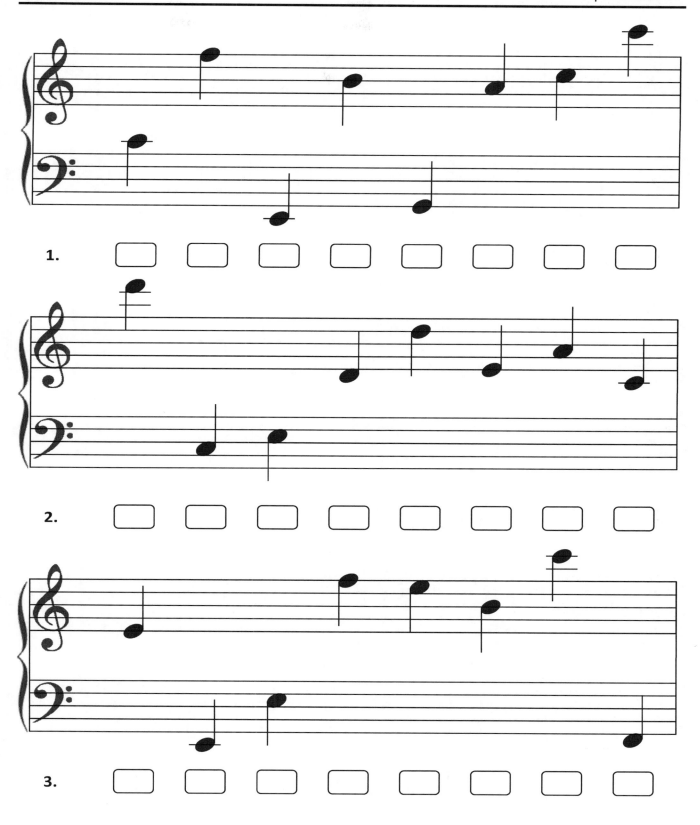

1. ☐ ☐ ☐ ☐ ☐ ☐ ☐ ☐

2. ☐ ☐ ☐ ☐ ☐ ☐ ☐ ☐

3. ☐ ☐ ☐ ☐ ☐ ☐ ☐ ☐

Completed On: _____   Number Correct: _____ / 24

1. ☐ ☐ ☐ ☐ ☐ ☐ ☐ ☐

2. ☐ ☐ ☐ ☐ ☐ ☐ ☐ ☐

3. ☐ ☐ ☐ ☐ ☐ ☐ ☐ ☐

Play me!

Completed On: _____   Number Correct: _____ / 24

1.

2.

3.

Completed On: _____   Number Correct: _____ / 24

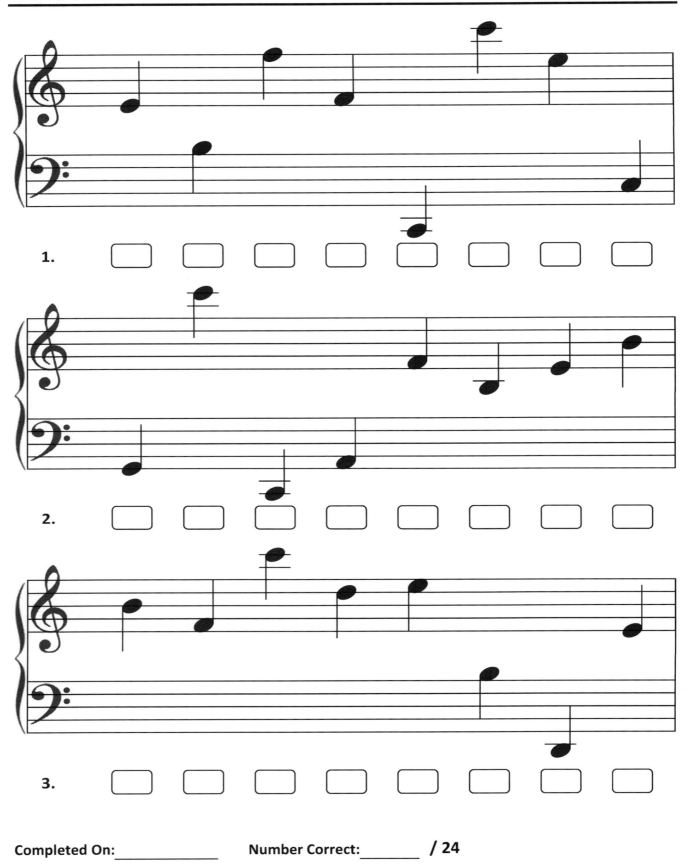

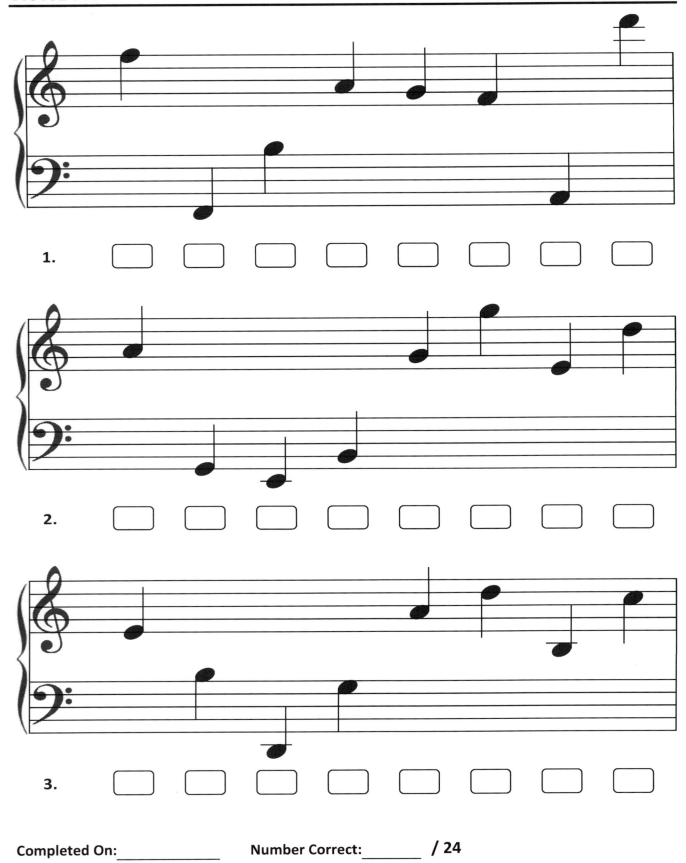

1.

2.

3.

Completed On: _____   Number Correct: _____ / 24   Play me!

Completed On: _____   **Number Correct:** _____ **/ 24**

1. ☐ ☐ ☐ ☐ ☐ ☐ ☐ ☐

2. ☐ ☐ ☐ ☐ ☐ ☐ ☐ ☐

3. ☐ ☐ ☐ ☐ ☐ ☐ ☐ ☐

Completed On: _____ Number Correct: _____ / 24

Completed On:_____   Number Correct:_____ / 24

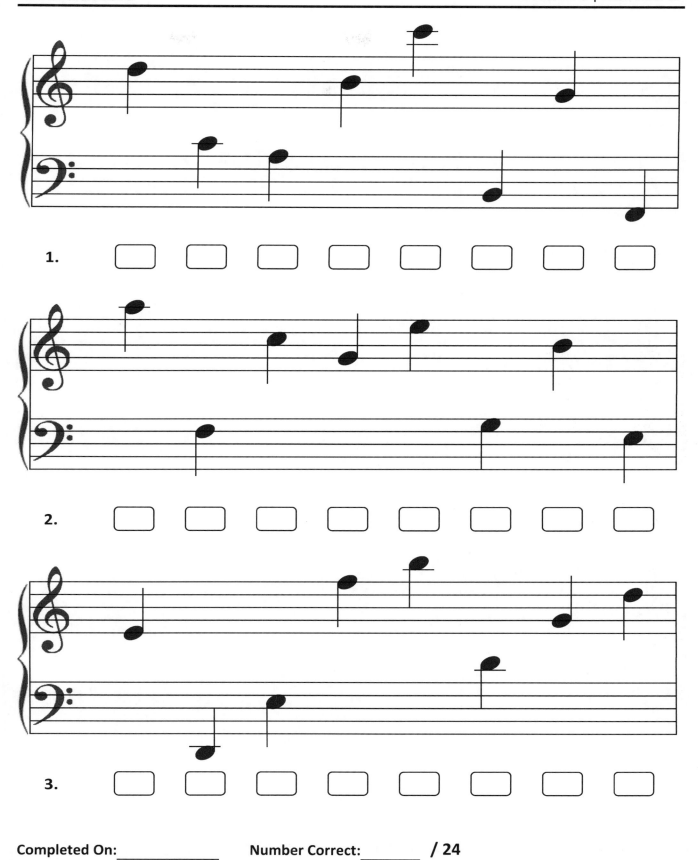

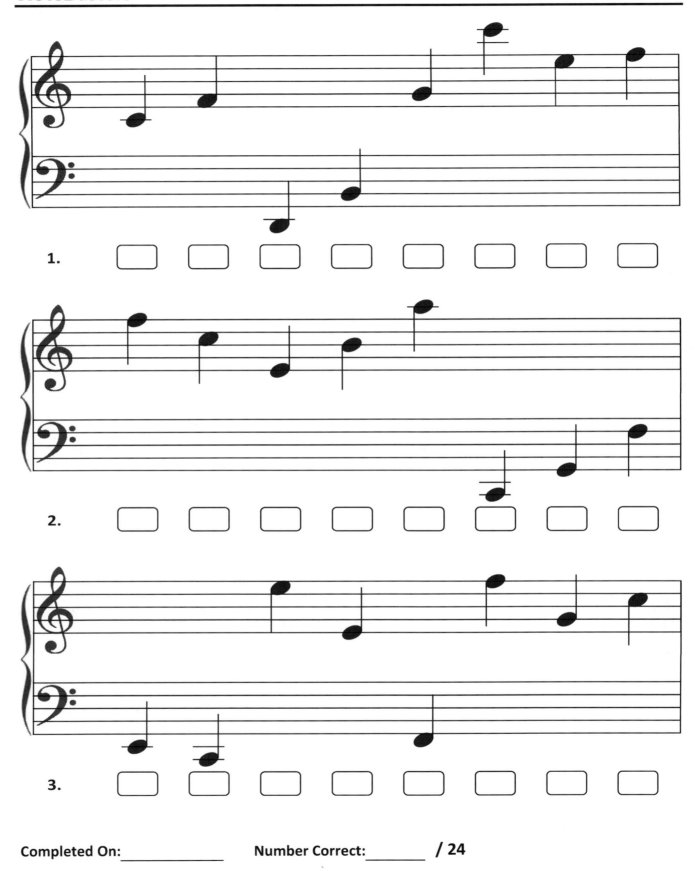

Completed On: _____   **Number Correct:** _____ **/ 24**

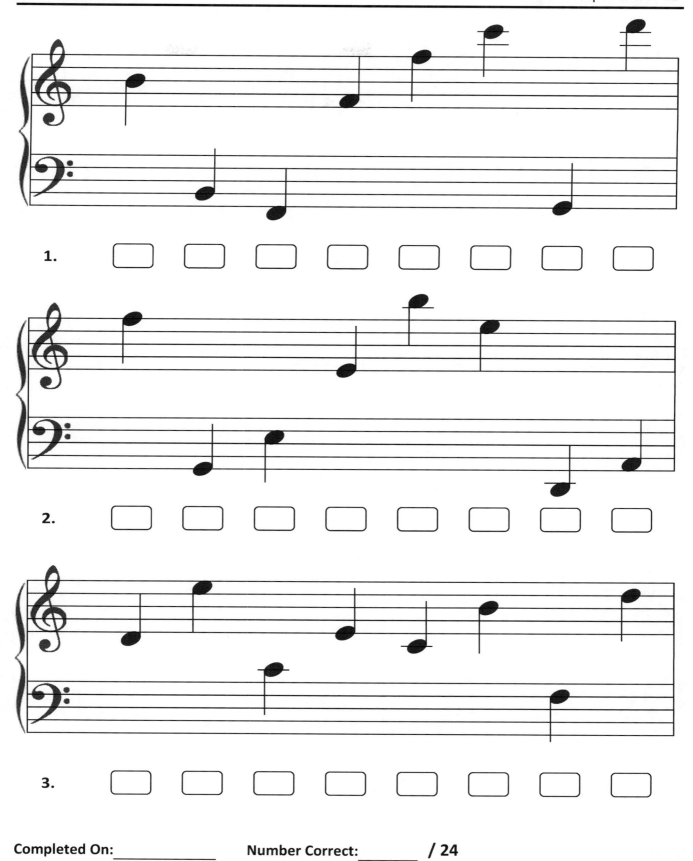

1.

2.

3.

Completed On: _____ **Number Correct:** _____ **/ 24**

Completed On: _____   Number Correct: _____ / 24

1.

2.

3.

Completed On: _____   Number Correct: _____ / 24   Play me!

Completed On: _____   Number Correct: _____ / 24

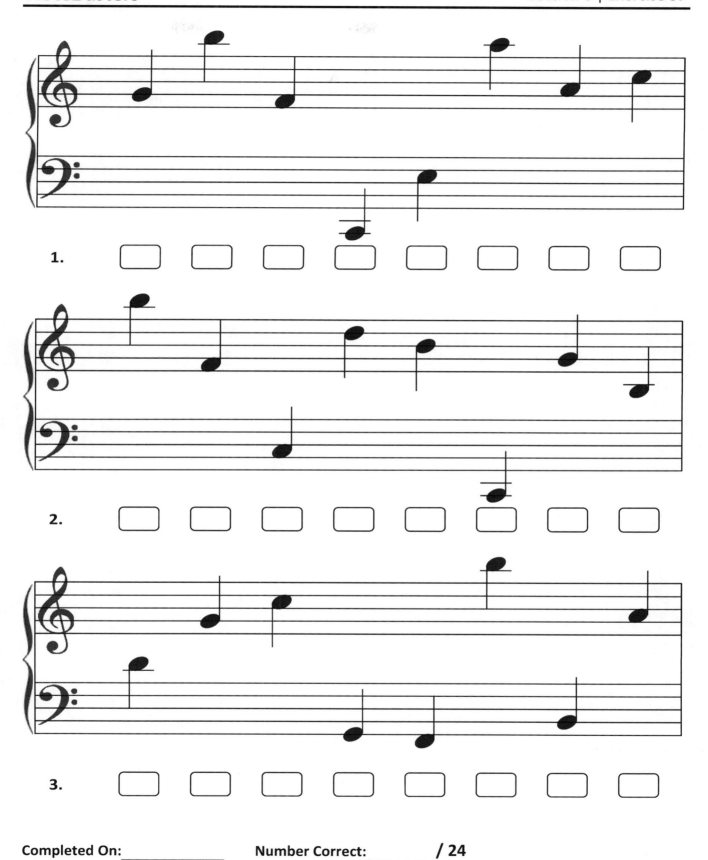

Completed On: _____

Number Correct: _____ / 24

1. ⬚ ⬚ ⬚ ⬚ ⬚ ⬚ ⬚ ⬚

2. ⬚ ⬚ ⬚ ⬚ ⬚ ⬚ ⬚ ⬚

3. ⬚ ⬚ ⬚ ⬚ ⬚ ⬚ ⬚ ⬚

Completed On: _____   Number Correct: _____ / 24

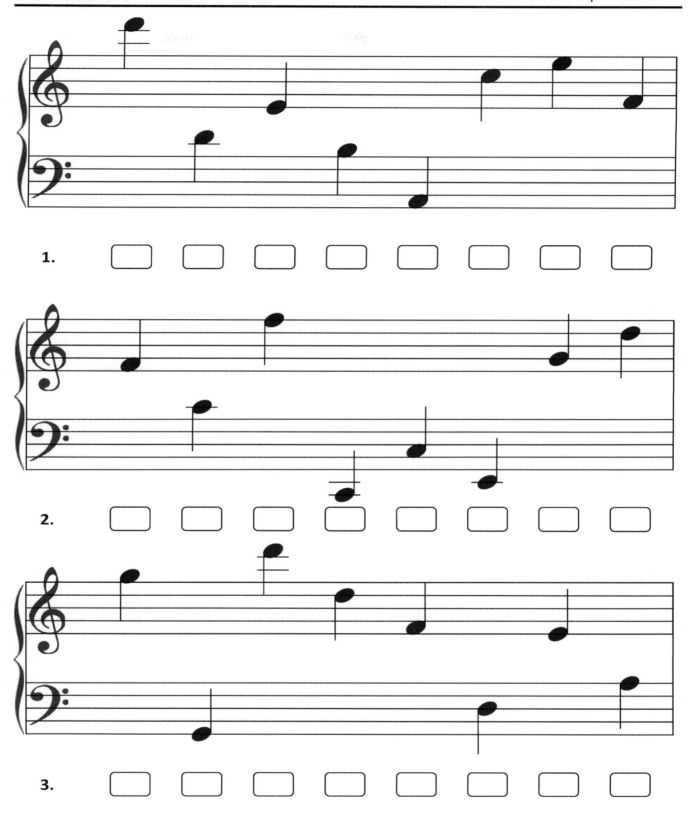

1. ☐ ☐ ☐ ☐ ☐ ☐ ☐ ☐

2. ☐ ☐ ☐ ☐ ☐ ☐ ☐ ☐

3. ☐ ☐ ☐ ☐ ☐ ☐ ☐ ☐

Completed On: _____   **Number Correct:** _____ **/ 24**

Completed On: _____   Number Correct: _____ / 24

Completed On: _____   Number Correct: _____ / 24

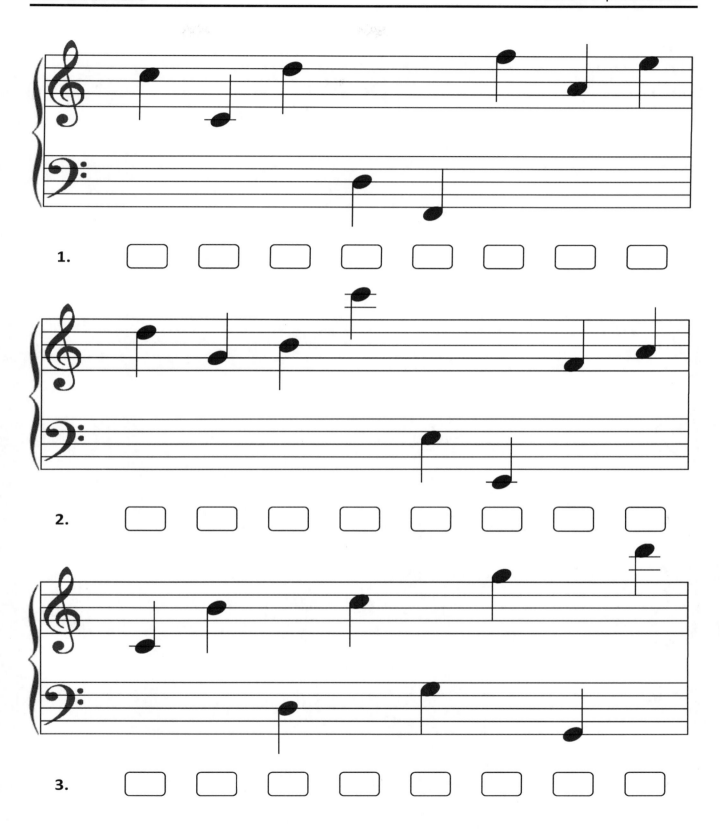

1.

2.

3.

Completed On: _____   Number Correct: _____ / 24

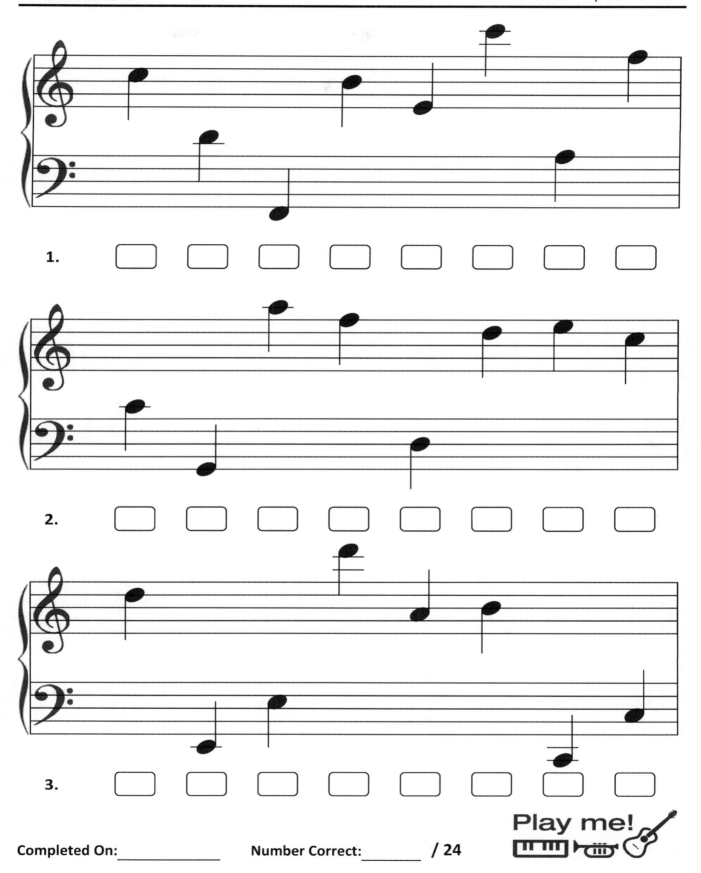

Play me!

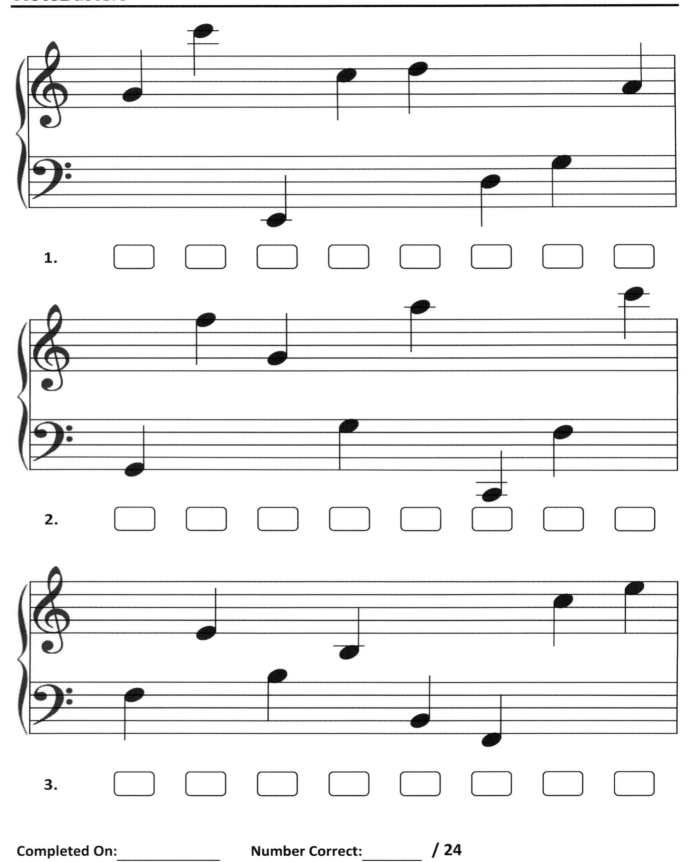

Completed On: _____   **Number Correct:** _____ **/ 24**

Completed On: _____ Number Correct: _____ / 24

1. ☐ ☐ ☐ ☐ ☐ ☐ ☐ ☐

2. ☐ ☐ ☐ ☐ ☐ ☐ ☐ ☐

3. ☐ ☐ ☐ ☐ ☐ ☐ ☐ ☐

Completed On: _____   **Number Correct:** _____ **/ 24**

Completed On: _____   Number Correct:_____ / 24

1.

2.

3.

Completed On: _____   Number Correct: _____ / 24   Play me!

1. ▢ ▢ ▢ ▢ ▢ ▢ ▢ ▢

2. ▢ ▢ ▢ ▢ ▢ ▢ ▢ ▢

3. ▢ ▢ ▢ ▢ ▢ ▢ ▢ ▢

Completed On: _____   **Number Correct:** _____ **/ 24**

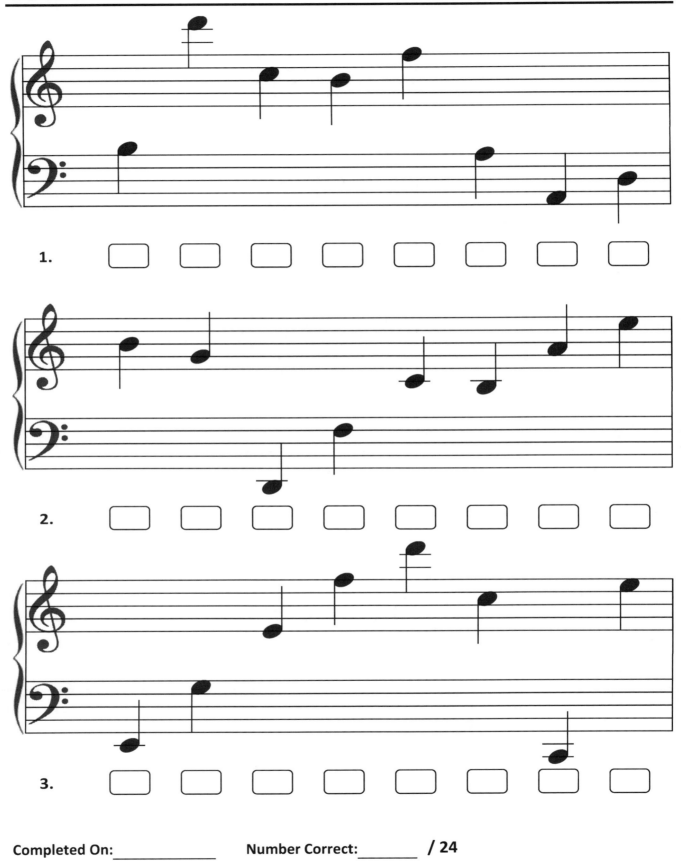

Completed On: _____   Number Correct: _____ / 24

1. ☐ ☐ ☐ ☐ ☐ ☐ ☐ ☐

2. ☐ ☐ ☐ ☐ ☐ ☐ ☐ ☐

3. ☐ ☐ ☐ ☐ ☐ ☐ ☐ ☐

Completed On: _____   Number Correct:_____ / 24

Completed On: _____   **Number Correct:** _____ **/ 24**

1.

2.

3.

Play me!

Completed On: _____   Number Correct: _____ / 24

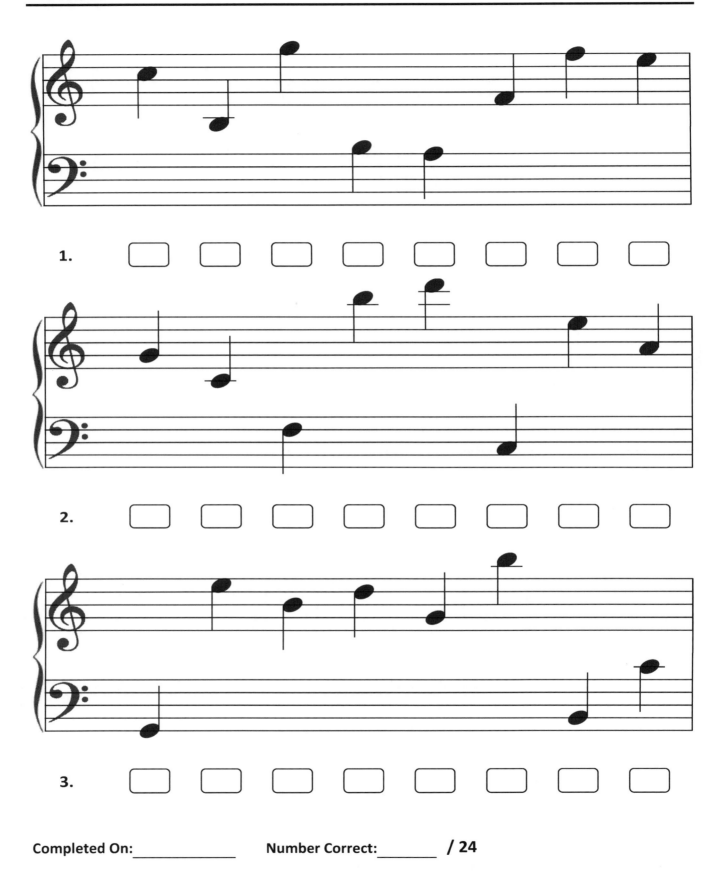

1.

2.

3.

Completed On: _____   **Number Correct:** _____ **/ 24**

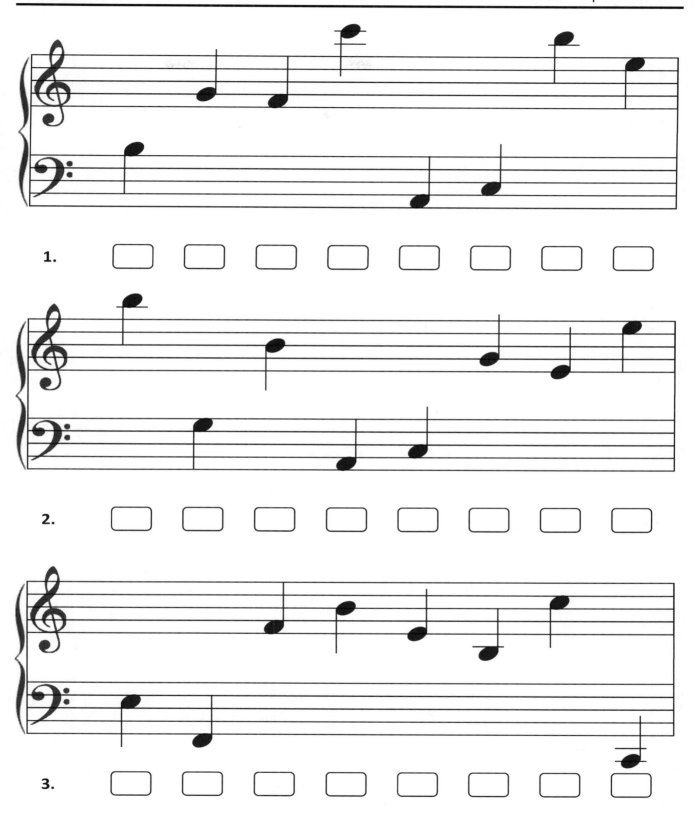

1.

2.

3.

Completed On: _____   Number Correct: _____ / 24

1. ☐ ☐ ☐ ☐ ☐ ☐ ☐ ☐

2. ☐ ☐ ☐ ☐ ☐ ☐ ☐ ☐

3. ☐ ☐ ☐ ☐ ☐ ☐ ☐ ☐

Completed On: _____   **Number Correct:** _____ **/ 24**

Completed On: _____   Number Correct: _____ / 24

Completed On: _____   Number Correct:_____ / 24

Play me!

Row	#1	#2	#3	#4	#5	#6	#7	#8
Section 1, Exercise 1								
1	G	F	E	A	C			
2	B	F	F	A	C			
3	G	F	E	B	A			
4	B	E	C	A	F			
5	F	B	G	D	E			
Section 1, Exercise 2								
1	F	B	A	G	E			
2	A	C	D	B	F			
3	F	C	F	E	G			
4	C	A	F	D	G			
5	F	A	C	E	D			
Section 1, Exercise 3								
1	A	C	E	B	D			
2	E	F	F	G	B			
3	F	E	D	G	E			
4	D	E	C	E	G			
5	G	E	E	C	A			
Section 1, Exercise 4								
1	E	A	D	C	G			
2	C	F	D	E	B			
3	D	A	E	C	B			
4	D	F	F	E	A			
5	F	E	F	C	A			
Section 1, Exercise 5								
1	G	D	C	F	E			
2	B	E	F	A	D			
3	E	D	E	F	A			
4	B	E	F	C	G			
5	A	F	D	C	E			
Section 1, Exercise 6								
1	D	F	B	C	A			
2	G	A	E	B	C			
3	B	E	F	A	C			
4	E	G	E	A	F			
5	C	F	D	B	F			
Section 1, Exercise 7								
1	E	E	G	D	F			
2	G	D	E	E	F			
3	A	G	D	F	F			
4	G	E	F	A	D			
5	F	B	A	D	F			

Row	#1	#2	#3	#4	#5	#6	#7	#8
Section 1, Exercise 8								
1	F	B	A	F	G			
2	F	E	F	E	A			
3	D	E	E	C	A			
4	G	E	F	B	A			
5	A	B	E	F	F			
Section 1, Exercise 9								
1	A	E	E	C	D			
2	A	E	F	F	E			
3	E	F	C	E	F			
4	G	D	B	F	C			
5	G	E	D	F	B			
Section 1, Exercise 10								
1	E	F	B	C	A			
2	A	B	E	G	C			
3	C	A	E	B	F			
4	F	E	G	E	C			
5	G	D	C	B	F			
Section 1, Exercise 11								
1	B	E	A	C	F			
2	D	G	F	F	B			
3	G	C	B	E	F			
4	C	D	F	E	F			
5	B	E	A	G	C			
Section 1, Exercise 12								
1	B	G	E	D	E			
2	E	C	B	A	E			
3	E	B	C	F	G			
4	E	D	G	B	E			
5	E	B	C	G	D			
Section 1, Exercise 13								
1	D	C	B	F	E			
2	B	E	F	E	F			
3	F	C	E	E	G			
4	E	F	F	C	B			
5	F	A	C	E	E			
Section 1, Exercise 14								
1	E	E	B	G	F			
2	G	D	B	C	A			
3	C	D	E	F	B			
4	C	A	E	B	G			
5	B	G	E	F	D			

Row	#1	#2	#3	#4	#5	#6	#7	#8
Section 1, Exercise 15								
1	D	F	G	A	B			
2	E	C	F	B	A			
3	E	D	A	E	C			
4	D	G	C	B	F			
5	D	A	E	F	F			
Section 1, Exercise 16								
1	B	F	A	E	D			
2	E	G	C	A	E			
3	E	C	E	A	B			
4	B	A	G	E	F			
5	G	E	B	D	A			
Section 1, Exercise 17								
1	E	A	C	F	D			
2	G	F	F	E	B			
3	F	G	F	E	B			
4	E	E	G	C	F			
5	G	C	F	A	E			
Section 1, Exercise 18								
1	G	C	A	E	F			
2	E	F	F	A	G			
3	F	B	E	C	E			
4	F	A	E	G	E			
5	A	E	F	D	C			
Section 1, Exercise 19								
1	G	F	B	A	E			
2	B	A	E	D	F			
3	B	E	F	C	D			
4	E	F	G	F	C			
5	A	C	E	B	E			
Section 1, Exercise 20								
1	A	F	D	E	B			
2	F	F	C	D	E			
3	C	F	A	E	D			
4	E	F	E	D	G			
5	E	F	C	B	E			
Section 2, Exercise 1								
1	A	G	D	F	A			
2	G	A	F	E	A			
3	G	A	A	B	D			
4	G	E	G	A	F			
5	D	G	F	C	B			

Row	#1	#2	#3	#4	#5	#6	#7	#8
Section 2, Exercise 2								
1	D	C	A	F	E			
2	D	A	E	A	G			
3	D	A	A	B	C			
4	A	C	B	G	E			
5	C	G	F	G	B			
Section 2, Exercise 3								
1	G	E	F	B	D			
2	B	G	F	D	C			
3	F	B	C	A	G			
4	G	A	E	A	G			
5	E	D	C	A	F			
Section 2, Exercise 4								
1	B	C	E	G	D			
2	G	F	D	B	A			
3	B	A	E	A	D			
4	G	B	G	A	F			
5	A	C	A	G	E			
Section 2, Exercise 5								
1	B	C	G	E	F			
2	E	B	A	C	D			
3	D	A	G	E	B			
4	G	G	D	B	F			
5	G	A	C	E	D			
Section 2, Exercise 6								
1	B	E	D	A	G			
2	A	E	D	A	B			
3	D	E	G	G	F			
4	C	G	F	G	A			
5	E	F	G	C	A			
Section 2, Exercise 7								
1	D	E	C	F	G			
2	G	F	G	E	B			
3	A	A	C	D	G			
4	A	E	G	F	B			
5	C	D	F	E	B			
Section 2, Exercise 8								
1	G	D	F	E	A			
2	B	C	G	E	A			
3	A	E	G	C	A			
4	G	F	G	A	E			
5	A	A	D	G	G			

Row	#1	#2	#3	#4	#5	#6	#7	#8
Section 2, Exercise 9								
1	A	F	A	C	D			
2	C	G	F	A	B			
3	F	A	B	E	G			
4	C	G	B	F	A			
5	F	G	D	C	E			
Section 2, Exercise 10								
1	G	E	B	A	D			
2	D	G	G	E	B			
3	G	A	G	E	A			
4	C	G	A	D	G			
5	B	G	G	A	C			
Section 2, Exercise 11								
1	F	G	E	D	B			
2	A	G	E	F	B			
3	C	G	A	F	E			
4	D	G	A	F	E			
5	B	A	C	E	G			
Section 2, Exercise 12								
1	B	A	C	G	F			
2	F	G	A	C	B			
3	G	G	A	D	E			
4	G	A	G	D	C			
5	A	F	D	A	G			
Section 2, Exercise 13								
1	B	D	A	E	F			
2	C	B	D	G	E			
3	E	A	C	B	D			
4	A	C	E	D	F			
5	G	A	D	B	A			
Section 2, Exercise 14								
1	A	A	F	B	G			
2	D	A	C	G	G			
3	C	G	E	A	A			
4	G	A	B	E	F			
5	E	G	D	A	G			
Section 2, Exercise 15								
1	E	A	G	F	D			
2	D	F	A	A	G			
3	D	G	A	B	G			
4	F	G	E	A	C			
5	G	A	D	G	B			

Row	#1	#2	#3	#4	#5	#6	#7	#8
Section 2, Exercise 16								
1	E	G	A	C	F			
2	A	A	F	D	G			
3	G	E	D	A	A			
4	C	E	F	G	D			
5	G	A	E	D	A			
Section 2, Exercise 17								
1	A	E	D	G	C			
2	B	E	A	A	F			
3	A	G	F	C	A			
4	B	G	A	F	D			
5	F	A	D	E	C			
Section 2, Exercise 18								
1	G	G	A	E	F			
2	E	C	D	G	A			
3	D	A	C	G	E			
4	C	A	B	G	G			
5	E	G	A	G	B			
Section 2, Exercise 19								
1	F	A	D	B	G			
2	G	G	C	A	B			
3	E	A	A	G	G			
4	G	G	B	D	E			
5	D	B	A	G	E			
Section 2, Exercise 20								
1	D	G	B	F	C			
2	F	A	D	G	B			
3	C	A	E	B	F			
4	F	D	B	E	A			
5	C	F	E	B	D			
Section 2, Exercise 21								
1	A	E	B	A	C			
2	G	C	F	G	B			
3	F	B	D	A	E			
4	F	A	B	C	G			
5	D	G	B	F	C			
Section 2, Exercise 22								
1	E	G	A	D	C			
2	F	B	E	D	C			
3	D	A	E	C	G			
4	F	A	D	A	G			
5	G	E	F	C	D			

Row	#1	#2	#3	#4	#5	#6	#7	#8
Section 2, Exercise 23								
1	F	A	E	D	G			
2	E	A	B	F	G			
3	A	F	G	B	D			
4	A	B	A	G	C			
5	F	A	D	C	E			
Section 2, Exercise 24								
1	E	B	F	D	C			
2	B	G	G	F	D			
3	B	A	D	F	G			
4	B	A	G	F	C			
5	G	F	A	A	C			
Section 2, Exercise 25								
1	F	A	D	E	A			
2	G	E	B	D	A			
3	C	A	D	G	A			
4	C	A	G	D	B			
5	B	A	A	D	E			
Section 2, Exercise 26								
1	A	F	D	G	G			
2	G	B	C	A	E			
3	A	E	D	A	B			
4	E	F	C	B	G			
5	F	G	A	G	C			
Section 2, Exercise 27								
1	G	A	C	E	D			
2	G	C	B	A	F			
3	F	D	B	C	A			
4	B	G	D	F	A			
5	A	B	D	G	C			
Section 2, Exercise 28								
1	G	E	A	D	F			
2	E	B	G	F	G			
3	F	A	C	E	G			
4	D	B	A	G	E			
5	A	G	G	B	A			
Section 2, Exercise 29								
1	C	E	A	A	D			
2	C	G	F	D	B			
3	G	D	A	E	C			
4	A	E	D	B	F			
5	C	E	B	A	G			

Row	#1	#2	#3	#4	#5	#6	#7	#8
Section 2, Exercise 30								
1	A	B	C	G	A			
2	B	A	A	G	F			
3	F	E	A	G	D			
4	D	C	F	A	G			
5	E	D	B	G	A			
Section 2, Exercise 31								
1	G	C	F	G	A			
2	G	G	D	F	A			
3	G	B	E	A	A			
4	D	E	G	A	A			
5	A	A	B	G	C			
Section 2, Exercise 32								
1	B	A	C	E	F			
2	B	A	E	C	A			
3	D	C	G	A	F			
4	E	C	G	F	A			
5	A	G	B	C	D			
Section 2, Exercise 33								
1	F	C	B	G	D			
2	B	G	A	G	F			
3	F	G	C	G	E			
4	F	D	A	G	B			
5	A	G	B	D	F			
Section 2, Exercise 34								
1	A	G	E	D	C			
2	G	E	C	A	A			
3	A	F	G	E	B			
4	D	E	A	G	C			
5	E	A	B	G	A			
Section 2, Exercise 35								
1	D	A	F	G	A			
2	D	F	C	B	E			
3	E	C	A	D	G			
4	F	A	D	G	C			
5	A	D	F	C	A			
Section 2, Exercise 36								
1	B	G	E	D	G			
2	G	E	C	D	A			
3	D	G	G	B	C			
4	B	A	D	E	C			
5	A	B	F	A	C			

Row	#1	#2	#3	#4	#5	#6	#7	#8
Section 2, Exercise 37								
1	F	C	D	A	E			
2	E	C	B	F	D			
3	B	A	F	G	C			
4	D	G	E	B	F			
5	G	A	C	D	F			
Section 2, Exercise 38								
1	F	G	B	C	E			
2	D	G	C	A	E			
3	G	G	A	B	F			
4	B	A	C	A	G			
5	A	G	G	C	A			
Section 2, Exercise 39								
1	A	G	F	B	C			
2	E	G	G	A	C			
3	E	D	G	A	C			
4	B	C	G	D	A			
5	A	A	D	B	E			
Section 2, Exercise 40								
1	G	E	D	G	B			
2	B	C	E	A	D			
3	A	A	G	E	G			
4	G	D	A	A	G			
5	G	B	C	E	G			
Section 3, Exercise 1								
1	D	F	F	C	A	G	A	E
2	A	D	B	C	C	G	G	A
3	G	F	A	E	B	A	F	F
Section 3, Exercise 2								
1	C	C	A	D	F	D	G	A
2	B	D	G	D	E	F	A	G
3	E	D	A	F	G	G	B	F
Section 3, Exercise 3								
1	G	C	C	F	A	E	D	E
2	B	E	A	G	E	A	F	D
3	B	A	C	E	G	E	D	E
Section 3, Exercise 4								
1	D	D	G	A	A	F	C	E
2	G	F	A	E	B	G	F	E
3	B	G	C	A	F	F	G	D
Section 3, Exercise 5								
1	F	A	G	D	G	F	C	E
2	F	D	G	C	B	A	E	E
3	A	G	D	E	F	C	E	F

Row	#1	#2	#3	#4	#5	#6	#7	#8
Section 3, Exercise 6								
1	D	F	E	E	E	A	C	F
2	G	E	C	B	G	D	B	E
3	C	F	C	B	E	A	A	F
Section 3, Exercise 7								
1	E	E	G	G	D	G	F	A
2	B	G	E	B	G	D	C	D
3	G	G	G	E	B	F	C	A
Section 3, Exercise 8								
1	B	F	C	B	D	G	F	E
2	D	D	B	F	F	F	E	C
3	F	E	A	E	D	G	F	C
Section 3, Exercise 9								
1	E	G	C	F	E	B	D	G
2	G	C	E	E	F	A	F	G
3	G	E	C	E	A	C	B	D
Section 3, Exercise 10								
1	G	E	F	D	C	G	E	A
2	G	A	D	A	C	B	D	E
3	E	E	B	D	F	G	A	C
Section 3, Exercise 11								
1	C	F	D	B	B	F	D	A
2	C	A	B	E	D	F	E	C
3	G	B	E	C	F	A	D	E
Section 3, Exercise 12								
1	C	E	F	B	G	A	G	C
2	B	B	D	C	A	C	D	F
3	A	A	G	D	F	E	C	F
Section 3, Exercise 13								
1	E	G	D	G	E	B	B	C
2	G	D	G	D	G	F	E	A
3	C	G	D	A	G	F	F	B
Section 3, Exercise 14								
1	A	A	E	F	E	G	D	C
2	B	D	F	A	C	E	G	E
3	A	G	F	F	D	D	F	G
Section 3, Exercise 15								
1	E	F	G	E	C	A	G	F
2	E	D	B	C	A	F	E	D
3	A	A	G	C	B	E	F	G
Section 3, Exercise 16								
1	A	E	B	E	D	D	G	C
2	A	C	F	E	F	C	F	B
3	D	A	F	E	G	A	F	E

Row	#1	#2	#3	#4	#5	#6	#7	#8
Section 3, Exercise 17								
1	A	D	G	D	E	C	E	F
2	C	B	E	C	F	F	G	F
3	D	C	C	A	D	B	B	E
Section 3, Exercise 18								
1	E	A	D	A	C	D	A	E
2	G	E	F	G	D	A	F	E
3	C	A	B	G	A	F	G	E
Section 3, Exercise 19								
1	F	A	E	E	C	E	B	F
2	A	F	A	F	G	D	E	G
3	B	E	F	F	F	A	G	G
Section 3, Exercise 20								
1	A	C	F	G	F	E	E	D
2	E	F	B	F	G	A	C	F
3	E	B	D	C	F	B	A	A
Section 3, Exercise 21								
1	E	B	F	C	E	D	D	E
2	E	B	A	D	A	C	C	F
3	E	F	G	A	G	E	B	C
Section 3, Exercise 22								
1	B	A	C	E	F	C	G	D
2	B	E	C	E	A	F	G	B
3	B	A	F	E	E	D	A	C
Section 3, Exercise 23								
1	E	A	B	G	D	E	F	D
2	F	F	G	E	A	G	E	G
3	D	G	A	G	C	D	E	F
Section 3, Exercise 24								
1	D	D	A	G	B	C	F	A
2	C	G	E	D	B	C	D	B
3	D	B	G	A	F	B	D	E
Section 3, Exercise 25								
1	G	F	B	C	A	F	E	D
2	G	D	E	C	F	F	C	B
3	A	B	E	C	G	F	F	A
Section 3, Exercise 26								
1	D	B	C	A	F	D	G	G
2	C	G	G	D	B	E	E	A
3	G	F	B	C	F	E	E	F
Section 3, Exercise 27								
1	F	B	D	E	A	D	G	A
2	F	E	E	C	G	A	A	F
3	B	E	F	C	A	G	G	F

Row	#1	#2	#3	#4	#5	#6	#7	#8
Section 3, Exercise 28								
1	E	C	A	E	D	C	F	B
2	E	A	B	E	G	G	D	F
3	A	E	E	E	A	F	C	D
Section 3, Exercise 29								
1	E	D	G	F	F	A	G	C
2	A	A	G	E	C	F	B	G
3	D	D	F	F	E	C	E	G
Section 3, Exercise 30								
1	G	E	C	F	A	A	F	D
2	G	B	A	C	A	C	D	F
3	C	G	D	F	B	E	F	G
Section 3, Exercise 31								
1	B	C	F	E	F	E	C	D
2	F	A	D	G	E	D	E	A
3	F	D	A	G	E	G	E	B
Section 3, Exercise 32								
1	E	B	D	G	F	A	E	A
2	G	F	A	E	D	G	D	C
3	E	E	B	G	F	A	A	B
Section 3, Exercise 33								
1	E	G	B	F	D	E	G	A
2	F	D	A	F	G	B	G	C
3	A	D	E	F	E	B	G	C
Section 3, Exercise 34								
1	G	A	D	E	C	E	B	E
2	G	B	D	F	E	A	C	A
3	G	E	E	G	B	C	A	G
Section 3, Exercise 35								
1	E	F	B	D	B	A	C	C
2	E	D	C	B	F	D	A	G
3	F	D	F	E	E	A	C	A
Section 3, Exercise 36								
1	G	G	E	C	B	F	D	D
2	E	G	E	E	C	G	A	D
3	A	B	F	A	E	C	F	E
Section 3, Exercise 37								
1	F	A	E	D	F	A	C	E
2	A	G	F	C	F	B	D	C
3	D	G	E	G	E	A	C	D
Section 3, Exercise 38								
1	E	F	B	E	F	A	D	C
2	E	G	D	E	C	B	G	C
3	G	E	D	D	G	F	F	E

Row	#1	#2	#3	#4	#5	#6	#7	#8
Section 3, Exercise 39								
1	D	D	E	C	G	F	G	B
2	C	E	G	D	C	A	B	G
3	A	F	D	B	F	D	G	A
Section 3, Exercise 40								
1	C	A	C	F	B	F	G	F
2	C	D	G	E	F	B	A	E
3	D	B	E	E	F	C	G	G
Section 4, Exercise 1								
1	F	E	B	F	C			
2	E	G	G	B	B			
3	F	C	E	C	A			
4	C	B	B	F	E			
5	A	F	D	B	D			
Section 4, Exercise 2								
1	E	D	B	A	G			
2	G	C	B	C	C			
3	F	C	B	B	D			
4	C	D	E	D	G			
5	A	E	E	D	G			
Section 4, Exercise 3								
1	A	G	C	G	E			
2	E	E	A	B	D			
3	F	C	A	F	B			
4	D	C	G	A	E			
5	D	G	F	D	B			
Section 4, Exercise 4								
1	A	E	A	B	D			
2	D	D	A	B	B			
3	C	F	G	B	B			
4	A	G	C	B	D			
5	D	E	F	F	B			
Section 4, Exercise 5								
1	C	G	D	F	B			
2	G	D	F	C	G			
3	B	E	A	C	B			
4	B	G	A	E	D			
5	D	F	D	C	F			
Section 4, Exercise 6								
1	E	G	A	F	G			
2	E	F	E	D	B			
3	F	A	G	D	E			
4	A	F	D	F	A			
5	D	F	G	A	C			

Row	#1	#2	#3	#4	#5	#6	#7	#8
Section 4, Exercise 7								
1	E	F	D	G	D			
2	G	C	C	C	F			
3	E	E	B	D	G			
4	F	F	C	E	A			
5	E	A	F	F	D			
Section 4, Exercise 8								
1	C	D	F	A	B			
2	A	C	B	B	E			
3	G	D	F	A	C			
4	A	E	D	E	D			
5	A	C	B	E	E			
Section 4, Exercise 9								
1	B	C	C	D	E			
2	A	G	A	D	B			
3	D	E	E	C	C			
4	D	C	A	B	B			
5	C	D	C	G	G			
Section 4, Exercise 10								
1	D	E	C	E	B			
2	B	B	B	D	C			
3	G	G	D	B	F			
4	F	D	E	B	F			
5	B	C	B	A	D			
Section 4, Exercise 11								
1	D	D	C	E	F			
2	C	A	A	B	E			
3	D	B	F	E	C			
4	B	E	C	A	F			
5	C	F	A	F	A			
Section 4, Exercise 12								
1	B	F	G	D	B			
2	A	C	D	F	C			
3	D	A	D	G	E			
4	C	C	E	D	B			
5	B	E	F	G	D			
Section 4, Exercise 13								
1	C	D	C	A	B			
2	B	C	B	E	G			
3	D	A	G	B	C			
4	B	B	A	D	C			
5	C	C	F	G	F			

Row	#1	#2	#3	#4	#5	#6	#7	#8
Section 4, Exercise 14								
1	E	B	D	B	F			
2	G	E	B	A	D			
3	B	G	C	D	B			
4	B	C	D	D	A			
5	B	G	A	E	D			
Section 4, Exercise 15								
1	E	C	A	C	F			
2	B	D	C	G	C			
3	A	G	A	D	B			
4	G	C	F	E	F			
5	A	C	B	D	G			
Section 4, Exercise 16								
1	C	F	B	F	E			
2	D	G	D	A	D			
3	B	C	F	E	E			
4	F	C	G	B	E			
5	G	A	B	D	B			
Section 4, Exercise 17								
1	E	C	E	A	D			
2	B	D	A	F	E			
3	D	D	C	D	F			
4	G	C	E	D	C			
5	C	E	D	A	C			
Section 4, Exercise 18								
1	C	F	B	A	D			
2	D	B	G	F	E			
3	E	E	B	D	D			
4	C	G	F	D	F			
5	E	E	F	C	G			
Section 4, Exercise 19								
1	B	E	F	F	D			
2	G	C	B	D	B			
3	E	D	A	A	B			
4	D	G	B	C	E			
5	D	E	E	B	G			
Section 4, Exercise 20								
1	C	D	B	B	C			
2	C	F	A	B	E			
3	D	B	E	C	B			
4	D	F	C	G	B			
5	B	A	C	C	D			

Row	#1	#2	#3	#4	#5	#6	#7	#8
Section 5, Exercise 1								
1	A	F	E	G	A			
2	G	C	F	D	E			
3	E	G	F	C	C			
4	A	G	D	C	D			
5	B	G	A	F	D			
Section 5, Exercise 2								
1	C	F	E	F	B			
2	D	E	F	B	D			
3	E	B	C	C	G			
4	F	D	C	G	G			
5	C	G	B	D	F			
Section 5, Exercise 3								
1	E	C	E	C	A			
2	D	F	C	F	E			
3	E	G	D	G	C			
4	F	C	E	D	G			
5	C	E	B	A	C			
Section 5, Exercise 4								
1	G	C	E	A	C			
2	D	F	E	D	B			
3	A	E	D	G	F			
4	E	D	A	C	B			
5	E	F	F	C	G			
Section 5, Exercise 5								
1	A	G	G	C	E			
2	C	E	G	C	F			
3	D	E	C	D	F			
4	F	G	E	A	B			
5	E	C	A	G	D			
Section 5, Exercise 6								
1	A	C	B	C	E			
2	D	A	G	D	E			
3	F	D	E	G	D			
4	D	G	D	A	E			
5	D	D	G	B	C			
Section 5, Exercise 7								
1	B	D	C	G	A			
2	A	E	F	G	D			
3	F	E	C	C	C			
4	G	A	C	D	F			
5	D	C	D	E	C			

Row	#1	#2	#3	#4	#5	#6	#7	#8
Section 5, Exercise 8								
1	C	D	F	G	D			
2	A	E	F	F	G			
3	A	B	E	E	D			
4	B	G	A	F	D			
5	F	F	C	A	D			
Section 5, Exercise 9								
1	G	A	F	D	C			
2	C	C	D	B	G			
3	A	B	D	F	F			
4	F	A	G	B	C			
5	G	F	D	C	B			
Section 5, Exercise 10								
1	B	D	A	G	F			
2	B	A	F	C	D			
3	A	F	F	B	D			
4	C	E	B	E	F			
5	C	B	C	D	G			
Section 5, Exercise 11								
1	B	C	G	G	F			
2	C	G	F	D	E			
3	G	D	E	B	C			
4	A	B	F	E	C			
5	D	A	E	C	B			
Section 5, Exercise 12								
1	G	F	E	D	B			
2	C	F	A	G	B			
3	F	C	C	E	B			
4	D	G	A	C	D			
5	B	G	B	A	G			
Section 5, Exercise 13								
1	D	A	E	F	F			
2	F	G	C	C	A			
3	D	F	G	E	A			
4	A	F	D	D	G			
5	E	A	D	F	A			
Section 5, Exercise 14								
1	A	C	D	C	F			
2	D	C	B	G	A			
3	D	A	D	C	C			
4	A	E	C	F	D			
5	C	A	D	D	C			

Row	#1	#2	#3	#4	#5	#6	#7	#8
Section 5, Exercise 15								
1	C	C	G	A	C			
2	E	B	C	A	B			
3	A	G	E	B	F			
4	F	G	D	C	E			
5	A	C	A	C	B			
Section 5, Exercise 16								
1	F	D	D	B	C			
2	G	A	D	D	E			
3	F	G	D	C	D			
4	C	A	B	F	B			
5	C	A	D	B	A			
Section 5, Exercise 17								
1	B	C	D	E	D			
2	C	C	E	B	F			
3	G	F	A	B	G			
4	D	A	A	G	C			
5	A	B	D	F	G			
Section 5, Exercise 18								
1	A	C	D	D	E			
2	C	A	F	A	B			
3	B	C	F	E	C			
4	D	A	C	B	F			
5	F	G	F	D	B			
Section 5, Exercise 19								
1	A	D	C	B	A			
2	F	B	F	A	C			
3	A	D	D	G	B			
4	D	A	F	D	G			
5	C	D	C	D	A			
Section 5, Exercise 20								
1	D	G	C	F	C			
2	B	E	D	G	C			
3	C	G	A	A	D			
4	D	A	B	D	C			
5	D	C	D	C	G			
Section 5, Exercise 21								
1	B	F	D	F	C			
2	E	D	C	F	A			
3	E	F	C	B	C			
4	G	E	C	D	C			
5	D	A	C	B	C			

Row	#1	#2	#3	#4	#5	#6	#7	#8
Section 5, Exercise 22								
1	A	C	D	C	G			
2	C	C	A	B	E			
3	F	G	C	C	A			
4	F	A	G	E	C			
5	D	F	A	B	D			
Section 5, Exercise 23								
1	A	A	F	C	D			
2	F	C	A	F	G			
3	E	G	A	C	E			
4	C	C	B	A	D			
5	A	A	C	G	D			
Section 5, Exercise 24								
1	D	E	D	G	B			
2	D	C	A	B	G			
3	A	B	D	F	F			
4	F	G	G	F	E			
5	G	D	C	D	A			
Section 5, Exercise 25								
1	C	D	G	C	C			
2	D	A	B	G	C			
3	C	A	G	B	C			
4	C	C	F	D	G			
5	G	C	B	D	E			
Section 5, Exercise 26								
1	D	C	C	F	A			
2	B	E	C	E	F			
3	C	F	G	A	C			
4	D	A	C	G	B			
5	E	B	F	C	C			
Section 5, Exercise 27								
1	D	E	F	B	D			
2	F	D	G	D	D			
3	C	D	G	G	C			
4	A	C	G	D	B			
5	G	A	B	G	C			
Section 5, Exercise 28								
1	E	D	C	A	G			
2	D	F	C	C	B			
3	C	C	B	C	A			
4	E	D	C	C	D			
5	A	E	B	G	B			

Row	#1	#2	#3	#4	#5	#6	#7	#8
Section 5, Exercise 29								
1	F	E	G	B	A			
2	C	A	G	D	F			
3	D	C	B	F	G			
4	A	F	E	E	F			
5	C	B	A	F	E			
Section 5, Exercise 30								
1	C	D	F	C	D			
2	D	B	C	A	D			
3	D	F	A	E	C			
4	C	G	E	D	C			
5	F	A	D	A	E			
Section 5, Exercise 31								
1	B	C	D	D	F			
2	D	A	F	E	B			
3	G	C	D	E	A			
4	C	D	C	F	E			
5	B	C	F	C	A			
Section 5, Exercise 32								
1	D	F	C	G	A			
2	D	D	C	F	E			
3	C	C	D	E	D			
4	G	C	E	G	B			
5	C	D	A	E	D			
Section 5, Exercise 33								
1	A	A	G	F	F			
2	C	E	E	A	A			
3	F	D	A	A	G			
4	G	E	B	B	D			
5	A	D	F	E	D			
Section 5, Exercise 34								
1	E	D	G	F	A			
2	A	C	E	G	A			
3	A	B	G	E	F			
4	D	A	F	D	C			
5	G	F	C	G	F			
Section 5, Exercise 35								
1	G	E	D	F	F			
2	D	B	B	F	F			
3	F	C	D	C	D			
4	C	F	F	A	D			
5	D	A	E	B	F			

NoteBusters

Appendix | Answer Key

Row	#1	#2	#3	#4	#5	#6	#7	#8
Section 5, Exercise 36								
1	G	C	D	A	C			
2	G	A	E	A	F			
3	D	B	D	E	A			
4	C	D	F	A	E			
5	C	B	F	A	C			
Section 5, Exercise 37								
1	E	B	B	E	D			
2	A	B	G	F	C			
3	D	E	C	G	C			
4	C	C	E	G	B			
5	C	A	E	D	D			
Section 5, Exercise 38								
1	F	A	B	C	B			
2	F	D	B	G	C			
3	F	A	C	E	C			
4	A	E	G	F	B			
5	G	D	B	F	F			
Section 5, Exercise 39								
1	D	G	C	B	D			
2	F	E	D	B	A			
3	E	F	A	D	G			
4	B	A	A	F	B			
5	D	E	B	A	C			
Section 5, Exercise 40								
1	C	F	B	C	D			
2	E	E	B	C	A			
3	A	D	D	G	D			
4	D	G	A	C	E			
5	E	G	E	G	F			
Section 6, Exercise 1								
1	F	C	D	E	C	C	A	G
2	C	F	C	E	D	G	F	D
3	B	G	F	F	E	A	A	C
Section 6, Exercise 2								
1	B	E	E	C	E	G	A	A
2	G	D	A	F	C	A	E	G
3	F	D	F	G	A	D	F	D
Section 6, Exercise 3								
1	A	D	A	B	F	C	C	A
2	F	F	A	G	D	A	D	B
3	B	C	F	G	B	D	B	D

274

Row	#1	#2	#3	#4	#5	#6	#7	#8
Section 6, Exercise 4								
1	F	C	B	D	C	F	E	F
2	G	C	G	C	G	A	A	F
3	D	D	G	B	C	C	B	E
Section 6, Exercise 5								
1	F	C	B	C	B	E	B	D
2	F	B	F	B	B	E	B	D
3	E	A	F	B	D	G	F	G
Section 6, Exercise 6								
1	B	E	A	E	G	E	B	C
2	F	F	D	D	B	G	D	F
3	D	E	B	F	B	A	E	D
Section 6, Exercise 7								
1	E	D	A	C	C	C	E	D
2	G	B	F	G	B	C	E	A
3	E	F	G	F	D	B	D	C
Section 6, Exercise 8								
1	B	G	E	C	D	F	B	A
2	A	B	B	C	G	D	F	B
3	G	A	E	F	E	D	A	B
Section 6, Exercise 9								
1	D	E	C	F	A	B	D	E
2	E	E	A	D	B	F	D	B
3	B	G	E	E	D	E	A	F
Section 6, Exercise 10								
1	A	D	E	D	B	A	G	C
2	E	D	C	G	A	G	F	G
3	B	A	C	B	C	E	F	G
Section 6, Exercise 11								
1	F	E	E	G	F	C	B	G
2	D	G	D	A	C	E	G	E
3	A	E	G	C	F	C	C	F
Section 6, Exercise 12								
1	G	C	C	C	D	F	D	F
2	C	C	A	A	F	B	B	E
3	D	F	D	D	B	F	C	F
Section 6, Exercise 13								
1	A	E	F	B	E	D	B	F
2	C	D	C	F	C	G	F	A
3	E	G	F	B	B	E	A	G
Section 6, Exercise 14								
1	E	E	G	C	D	C	C	F
2	A	G	D	G	D	G	E	B
3	C	A	E	C	D	E	A	B

275

Row	#1	#2	#3	#4	#5	#6	#7	#8
Section 6, Exercise 15								
1	B	E	G	F	C	E	C	A
2	B	D	C	B	E	E	F	C
3	D	C	E	G	B	F	C	G
Section 6, Exercise 16								
1	F	F	A	C	D	C	D	F
2	D	A	C	E	E	G	E	F
3	D	B	F	G	E	D	D	A
Section 6, Exercise 17								
1	A	F	F	C	E	F	D	D
2	C	G	E	F	D	A	C	E
3	G	E	E	B	A	F	C	C
Section 6, Exercise 18								
1	E	B	G	B	G	F	D	A
2	G	F	C	D	C	A	F	G
3	F	C	E	E	C	A	A	D
Section 6, Exercise 19								
1	D	E	B	E	A	A	D	D
2	F	A	A	B	G	F	D	B
3	E	D	B	B	G	C	A	D
Section 6, Exercise 20								
1	B	D	C	C	G	A	D	D
2	F	C	B	C	B	A	A	G
3	A	A	G	C	C	G	E	C
Section 6, Exercise 21								
1	G	A	A	E	B	C	C	F
2	G	B	F	A	E	F	B	C
3	G	B	D	F	A	A	C	E
Section 6, Exercise 22								
1	F	E	E	C	A	D	E	B
2	G	D	C	C	F	F	C	D
3	E	B	D	B	E	A	A	F
Section 6, Exercise 23								
1	E	A	B	A	B	F	A	C
2	D	A	C	F	C	C	G	C
3	C	E	F	G	D	C	D	A
Section 6, Exercise 24								
1	E	C	F	C	A	G	G	G
2	C	E	B	G	F	B	A	F
3	E	D	D	E	G	F	B	E
Section 6, Exercise 25								
1	F	C	A	D	C	B	A	F
2	B	F	A	G	F	C	D	B
3	A	G	C	D	A	B	F	D

Row	#1	#2	#3	#4	#5	#6	#7	#8
Section 6, Exercise 26								
1	A	E	B	C	C	E	A	D
2	D	G	E	C	F	B	F	G
3	D	B	B	B	A	A	D	A
Section 6, Exercise 27								
1	A	B	F	F	D	C	C	A
2	D	A	G	F	C	G	C	B
3	D	A	A	C	D	E	D	G
Section 6, Exercise 28								
1	F	C	E	G	D	C	D	E
2	D	C	F	F	D	A	D	C
3	F	F	B	B	B	C	F	C
Section 6, Exercise 29								
1	C	G	D	E	A	G	F	C
2	E	B	C	D	F	G	F	D
3	G	B	G	D	A	A	D	G
Section 6, Exercise 30								
1	C	E	A	G	C	C	A	G
2	G	D	F	G	A	E	F	B
3	D	G	C	G	F	B	E	A
Section 6, Exercise 31								
1	E	D	A	F	A	F	B	E
2	D	E	B	F	E	A	C	E
3	F	C	E	B	D	E	G	C
Section 6, Exercise 32								
1	C	B	B	E	A	E	E	E
2	C	B	A	G	C	C	G	B
3	G	A	B	F	C	E	B	F
Section 6, Exercise 33								
1	G	B	F	G	D	C	D	G
2	G	A	E	G	C	C	G	B
3	E	F	F	D	D	A	E	F
Section 6, Exercise 34								
1	G	D	F	E	B	F	C	C
2	C	A	F	A	B	F	B	E
3	G	G	C	E	C	B	C	D
Section 6, Exercise 35								
1	E	F	F	A	B	E	F	B
2	D	A	A	F	G	B	E	B
3	C	F	G	E	E	C	B	A
Section 6, Exercise 36								
1	B	B	F	C	D	G	A	A
2	D	F	A	C	C	F	B	F
3	F	B	D	G	D	C	E	D

Row	#1	#2	#3	#4	#5	#6	#7	#8
Section 6, Exercise 37								
1	C	F	C	A	F	E	D	B
2	E	D	A	F	F	C	B	E
3	D	C	A	D	B	G	F	B
Section 6, Exercise 38								
1	E	A	C	B	G	F	D	D
2	C	C	F	C	B	G	D	A
3	C	G	A	B	C	E	B	D
Section 6, Exercise 39								
1	C	F	E	B	G	A	C	C
2	D	C	E	D	D	E	A	C
3	E	E	E	F	E	B	C	F
Section 6, Exercise 40								
1	F	D	G	A	F	A	B	C
2	A	C	G	G	D	B	D	F
3	A	F	E	B	C	F	C	B
Section 6, Exercise 41								
1	A	D	C	F	E	B	D	D
2	D	F	A	A	G	D	B	C
3	G	E	F	A	D	D	A	C
Section 6, Exercise 42								
1	E	B	F	F	C	C	E	C
2	G	C	C	A	F	B	E	B
3	B	F	C	D	E	B	D	E
Section 6, Exercise 43								
1	B	E	D	E	C	B	G	D
2	E	A	A	B	G	F	F	B
3	F	G	B	C	F	G	F	D
Section 6, Exercise 44								
1	F	F	B	A	G	F	A	D
2	A	G	E	B	G	G	E	D
3	E	B	D	G	A	D	B	C
Section 6, Exercise 45								
1	F	F	C	E	D	E	A	B
2	A	F	E	C	B	G	G	C
3	G	C	G	D	C	F	F	B
Section 6, Exercise 46								
1	F	A	E	F	G	C	D	G
2	E	C	F	C	C	D	C	F
3	A	C	G	C	D	G	D	B
Section 6, Exercise 47								
1	C	F	F	G	C	B	E	D
2	D	E	D	F	C	A	B	E
3	C	B	A	E	E	B	G	C

Row	#1	#2	#3	#4	#5	#6	#7	#8
Section 6, Exercise 48								
1	D	B	D	G	C	G	F	B
2	D	F	B	G	C	C	E	C
3	D	G	B	C	E	C	F	G
Section 6, Exercise 49								
1	D	C	A	B	C	B	G	F
2	A	F	C	G	E	G	B	E
3	E	D	E	F	B	D	G	D
Section 6, Exercise 50								
1	D	A	E	B	E	F	D	B
2	F	E	D	D	D	C	B	G
3	F	F	G	E	C	D	B	E
Section 6, Exercise 51								
1	C	D	E	A	B	B	F	A
2	A	F	B	B	E	G	G	C
3	E	D	D	C	G	C	E	A
Section 6, Exercise 52								
1	C	F	D	B	G	C	E	F
2	F	C	E	B	A	C	G	F
3	E	C	E	E	F	F	G	C
Section 6, Exercise 53								
1	B	B	F	F	F	C	G	D
2	F	G	E	E	B	E	D	A
3	D	E	C	E	C	B	F	D
Section 6, Exercise 54								
1	C	B	B	E	C	F	C	F
2	E	G	C	A	C	A	E	F
3	G	E	D	B	D	A	C	E
Section 6, Exercise 55								
1	C	D	C	C	E	G	A	F
2	E	C	B	F	D	D	A	F
3	C	B	C	D	C	E	E	E
Section 6, Exercise 56								
1	A	C	A	D	C	D	F	G
2	A	B	G	G	A	E	D	F
3	G	A	C	F	E	B	C	D
Section 6, Exercise 57								
1	G	B	F	C	E	A	A	C
2	B	F	C	D	B	C	G	B
3	D	G	C	G	F	B	B	A
Section 6, Exercise 58								
1	B	B	E	D	A	G	F	G
2	G	C	A	B	F	E	B	G
3	E	D	D	D	E	E	F	E

Row	#1	#2	#3	#4	#5	#6	#7	#8
Section 6, Exercise 59								
1	D	D	E	B	A	C	E	F
2	F	C	F	C	C	E	G	D
3	G	G	D	D	F	D	E	A
Section 6, Exercise 60								
1	D	B	A	D	F	C	A	A
2	E	E	A	D	C	D	C	G
3	F	G	G	D	A	C	A	C
Section 6, Exercise 61								
1	B	E	B	G	C	E	D	F
2	E	E	C	G	C	G	C	D
3	G	E	B	A	A	D	A	F
Section 6, Exercise 62								
1	A	E	G	E	C	D	C	E
2	A	G	F	B	E	E	C	D
3	B	C	E	D	D	D	B	G
Section 6, Exercise 63								
1	C	C	D	D	F	F	A	E
2	D	G	B	C	E	E	F	A
3	C	B	D	C	G	G	G	D
Section 6, Exercise 64								
1	A	C	E	A	E	B	F	C
2	D	B	D	F	C	A	E	E
3	A	D	A	B	C	E	G	E
Section 6, Exercise 65								
1	C	D	F	B	E	C	A	F
2	C	G	A	F	D	D	E	C
3	D	E	E	D	A	B	C	C
Section 6, Exercise 66								
1	G	C	E	C	D	D	G	A
2	G	F	G	G	A	C	F	C
3	F	E	B	B	B	F	C	E
Section 6, Exercise 67								
1	F	D	B	E	C	G	D	D
2	G	C	F	C	B	C	D	A
3	G	G	F	B	F	A	E	D
Section 6, Exercise 68								
1	G	C	D	B	C	E	G	B
2	B	D	B	A	E	E	F	E
3	F	A	C	E	F	B	B	C
Section 6, Exercise 69								
1	C	E	B	G	C	F	C	G
2	F	C	G	G	C	C	E	E
3	A	G	D	C	D	E	C	D

Row	#1	#2	#3	#4	#5	#6	#7	#8
Section 6, Exercise 70								
1	C	D	A	F	B	E	E	D
2	D	C	A	B	E	F	A	F
3	E	D	C	C	A	G	F	B
Section 6, Exercise 71								
1	D	C	A	G	D	E	G	G
2	A	C	F	D	G	G	D	E
3	D	A	G	D	B	F	D	G
Section 6, Exercise 72								
1	B	D	C	B	F	A	A	D
2	B	G	D	F	C	B	A	E
3	E	G	E	F	D	C	C	E
Section 6, Exercise 73								
1	E	D	C	F	E	D	G	A
2	B	C	E	D	C	G	E	F
3	A	B	C	E	F	C	D	D
Section 6, Exercise 74								
1	C	D	B	B	F	D	D	C
2	B	C	C	C	A	D	E	F
3	D	F	B	D	B	F	A	F
Section 6, Exercise 75								
1	C	B	C	B	F	G	D	A
2	F	G	B	E	A	D	G	F
3	A	B	D	F	B	C	C	A
Section 6, Exercise 76								
1	C	B	G	B	A	F	F	E
2	G	C	F	B	D	C	E	A
3	G	E	B	D	G	B	B	C
Section 6, Exercise 77								
1	B	G	F	C	A	C	B	E
2	B	G	B	A	C	G	E	E
3	E	F	F	B	E	B	C	C
Section 6, Exercise 78								
1	C	G	A	F	D	F	F	B
2	F	A	B	C	B	G	E	B
3	F	C	C	E	C	G	A	E
Section 6, Exercise 79								
1	E	A	F	D	F	A	B	D
2	D	C	B	B	D	F	G	D
3	B	F	F	E	F	A	C	D
Section 6, Exercise 80								
1	B	E	C	A	G	E	E	G
2	F	E	D	G	G	C	B	A
3	A	A	E	D	D	F	F	F

61171197R00160

Made in the USA
Charleston, SC
19 September 2016